Champions Wanted

DIRECTIONS IN DEVELOPMENT
Trade

Champions Wanted

Promoting Exports in the Middle East and North Africa

Mélise Jaud and Caroline Freund

WORLD BANK GROUP

Contents

Map

Tables

Acknowledgments

This report is a truly collective effort. It draws from a collection of background papers by economists from and outside the Middle East and North Africa (MENA) region, within and outside the World Bank.

The research papers were developed under the "Exporters in MENA" project led by Mélise Jaud (task team leader), under the direction of Caroline Freund, senior fellow at the Peterson Institute for International Economics and in collaboration with Ahmed Galal, Rana Hendy, and Chahir Zaki at the Economic Research Forum (ERF) in Cairo. The authors thank Shantayanan Devarajan, Chief Economist of the World Bank MENA region, for his comments, guidance, and encouragement during the course of preparing this report.

We are grateful to the researchers for their contributions but also for creating a stimulating environment that helped the authors shape and prepare the report. Background papers were prepared by Hassan Arouri (INS Tunis), Alan Asprilla (University of Lausanne), Patricia Augier (University of Aix-Marseille), Leila Baghdadi (Tunis Business School), Nicolas Berman (HEI Geneva), Brian Blankespoor (World Bank), Florian Le Bris (Paris School of Economics), Claire Brunel (American University), Olivier Cadot (University of Lausanne), Anne-Celia Disdier (Paris School of Economics), Marion Dovis (University of Aix-Marseille), Hoda El-Enbaby (ERF), Ana Fernandes (World Bank), Julien Gourdon (OECD), Jamal Haidar (Paris School of Economics), Rana Hendy (ERF), Youssouf Kiendrebeogo (World Bank), Tobias Lechtenfeld (World Bank), Jaime de Melo (University of Geneva), Antonio Nucifora (World Bank), Marcelo Olarreaga (University of Geneva), Martha Pierola (World Bank), Gael Raballand (World Bank), Bob Rijkers (World Bank), Natalie Scholl (University of Göttingen), Akiko Suwa-Eisenmann (Paris School of Economics), Cristian Ugarte (UNCTAD), Roy Van der Weide (World Bank), Christina Wood (World Bank), Judy Yang (World Bank), Chahir Zaki (University of Cairo), and Laura Zoratto (World Bank).[1]

We particularly thank our reviewers, Paulo Bastos (World Bank), Mouna Cherkaoui (University Mohamed V), Ndiame Diop (World Bank), Mary Hallward-Driemeier (World Bank), Hanan Morsy (EBRD), and Khalid Sekkat (Free University of Brussels), for their very helpful and constructive suggestions. The report also benefited immensely from inputs, discussions, and suggestions from Olivier Cadot and Ana Fernandes.

In addition, the report benefited from specific comments and discussions with colleagues from the World Bank, Jean-Pierre Chauffour, Bernard Funck, Elena Ianchovichina, Farruh Iqbal, Mariem Malouche, Daniela Marotta, Aaditya Mattoo, Lili Motaghi, Mustapha Rouis, Sebastian Saez, Nikola Spatafora, Marc Schiffbauer, and Abdoulaye Sy. Finally, the team gained much from the inputs of the participants in the authors' workshops held at the World Bank in Washington, DC, in December 2013; the policy event held at the 20th ERF annual conference in Cairo, in March 2014; as well as in the CSAE 2014 conference in Oxford, in March 2014.

This report would not have been possible without the access to the firm-level data. For this we would like to thank Ana Fernandes and Denisse Pierola for providing access to the Exporter Dynamics Database as well as providing firm-level data for a number of non-MENA countries. We would like to express our appreciation to Jamal Haidar for his extensive effort and help in collecting the customs firm-level data for the Islamic Republic of Iran, Jordan, Kuwait, and the Republic of Yemen. We also thank Maurizio Bussolo and Ndiame Diop for their help in collecting the data for Morocco and Lebanon, respectively. We also wish to express our thanks to the statistics and research institutions across the region that facilitated access to the data, including the Institut National de la Statistique in Tunisia; the Ministry of Planning and International Coordination, the Department of Statistics, and the Jordan Enterprise Development Corporation in Jordan; the Central Agency for Public Mobilization and Statistics in the Arab Republic of Egypt; the Customs departments in the Islamic Republic of Iran, Kuwait, Lebanon, Morocco, and the Republic of Yemen; and the Economic Research Forum.

Our thanks go to Isabelle Chaal-Dabi and Nathalie Lenoble, who provided outstanding administrative support throughout the project and preparation of the report. We would like to thank Niamh O'Sullivan, who did an excellent job on editing the report, and to Aziz Gökdemir and Paola Scalabrin in the World Bank's Publishing and Knowledge department, who brilliantly coordinated the overall report production. Finally, the financial support of the MENA regional funds and the Multi-Donor Trade Trust Fund is gratefully acknowledged.

Note

1. Background papers presented during the authors' workshop can be accessed at the following address: http://web.worldbank.org/WBSITE/EXTERNAL/COUNTRIES /MENAEXT/0,,contentMDK:23503794~menuPK:9464020~pagePK:146736~piPK :146830~theSitePK:256299,00.html.

About the Authors

Mélise Jaud is an economist in the Chief Economist's Office of the World Bank's Middle East and North Africa Region. Her research covers international trade, in particular the determinants and impacts of firms' export dynamics and growth, food safety issues in trade, and policy reforms in developing and transition countries. Prior to joining the World Bank she worked as an economic advisor to the Ministry of Agriculture in Mozambique. She received her PhD in economics from the Paris School of Economics.

Caroline Freund is a senior fellow at the Peterson Institute for International Economics. Prior to that she was chief economist for the Middle East and North Africa Region at the World Bank. She has also worked in the research departments of the World Bank, the International Monetary Fund, and the Federal Reserve Board. Freund works primarily on economic growth and international trade and also writes on economic issues in the Middle East and North Africa. She has published numerous articles in economics journals, including *American Economic Review*, *Quarterly Journal of Economics*, *Review of Economics and Statistics*, *Journal of International Economics*, *Journal of International Money and Finance*, and *Journal of Development Economics*, and has contributed to many edited volumes. She is on the scientific committees of CEPII (Institute for Research of the International Economy, Paris) and the Economic Research Forum (Cairo), and is a member of the US Export-Import Bank Advisory Committee and of the Center for Economic Policy Research.

Overview

Traditional discussions of export performance are typically cast in terms of countries and sectors—which has a comparative advantage, what should be protected, and so on. Yet, neither countries nor sectors trade; firms do. By exploiting a rich, firm-level data set on exporters in the Middle East and North Africa (MENA), this report sheds new evidence on a number of old questions—ranging from the effects of exchange rate policy to market structure to export promotion to industrial policy—where a firm-level perspective makes it possible to move beyond well-worn diagnoses and debates. While the findings in this report have implications beyond MENA, they have particular salience to the region where job creation and economic growth have never been more urgent.

Based on the new data, evidence reported in this report provides new perspectives on how policy affects trade costs and market structure. Carrying out the analysis at the level of the firm makes it possible to identify these effects through largely unexplored adjustment margins like pricing or the breadth of product and destination portfolios. Moreover, the very fine level of disaggregation of the data allows us to estimate for "within-firm" effects, filtering out many confounding influences. This improves substantially the quality of inference and allows for more robust evaluation of policy impacts and ultimately policy prescriptions.

The central finding is that the size distribution of MENA's exporting firms is suggestive of a critical weakness at the top. MENA has champions (the individual firms at the top of the distributions) of a size comparable to other regions, but it lacks teams of world-class exporters to surround and emulate the "number ones." Its top 1 percent exporters are significantly smaller, on average, than in other regions. Thus, MENA countries have failed to nurture a group of export champions which critically contribute to export success in other regions.

Small size means that MENA's champions do not punch as heavily as they should. This report uses a novel approach to the measurement of market power, relying on recent theoretical advances linking pricing-to-market behavior at the firm level to the extent of market power. Identifying pricing to market through the adjustment of producer prices to exchange-rate shocks, we show that MENA exporters lack market power on their destination markets compared to a control group of exporters from other developing or emerging regions. Being price takers is a consequence of being too small.

It may also be a consequence of insufficient innovation and drive. In other regions, the largest exporters lead the way in terms of specialization. That is, there is a close correlation between the prevalence of export superstars and the degree of sector-level comparative advantage. Not so in MENA, where the correlation is weaker, suggesting that large-firm strategies may reflect, at least partly, a legacy of distorted incentives.

These idiosyncratic features of MENA's exporter population reflect a combination of structural and policy-induced factors. One is the well-known issue of an over-valued real exchange rate. The recent literature provides a wealth of evidence on the inhibiting effects of overvalued currencies on firm-level expansion of trade volumes and introduction of new products into new markets, with insights directly applicable to MENA. There is also the combination of tough, competitive European Union (EU) markets at the region's doorstep, with poor, restrictive domestic environments, which makes for a formidable gap to jump over.

In view of the region's acute job problem, the costs of MENA's failure to develop effective export champions are potentially high. Thousands of new young people enter the labor force each year, and in the region's volatile political environment, responding to their demands is crucial. Exporting firms, in particular in the manufacturing sector, hold the answer; they provide more and higher quality jobs, raising the return to education, and spreading the benefits of growth. Providing these firms with the right enabling environment is the region's key policy challenge.

Where does this lead us in terms of policy prescriptions? The report re-visits several traditional questions from the perspective of firms. First, there is no successful exporting without successful importing. The report provides strong, firm-level evidence that export performance correlates with the quality of imported intermediaries. While subcontractors in global value chains (GVC), being part of coordinated trans-frontier structures, incur no search costs, for independent mid-size companies, identifying reliable overseas suppliers can be a challenge. The region's governments should break from their traditional logic of "export, do not import" and instead facilitate all firms' access to imported inputs.

The report also highlights the role that regulatory reform can play in enhancing firm competitiveness. Morocco's regulatory harmonization with the EU while far from complete, provides an interesting natural experiment to assess how tougher but modernized regulations affect firm performance. Contrary to widely-held views, tougher regulations, such as imposing hygienic practices during production or traceability requirements, do not necessarily hurt the competitiveness of domestic firms. They can have a "clean-up" effect on the domestic market by keeping out lower-end suppliers, providing better incentives to upgrade quality. They can also help overcome managerial failures and encourage companies to innovate (Porter 1991; Porter and van der Linde 1995).

Sluggish export performance makes it tempting for governments in MENA to resort to industrial policy, in spite of the weak track record of State intervention in the region. Analysis of MENA's prevalent cronyism and corruption under pre-Arab Spring regimes confirms that business-government ties led to distortionary allocation of favors and rent dissipation by beneficiary firms, with little evidence that those firms developed into national champions or helped lift the region's export performance. This in itself should call for caution when advocating any form of government intervention.

However, while the potential for capture and government failures is large, some forms of clinical intervention, like export promotion, seem to work. For instance, a recent impact evaluation of Tunisia's FAMEX program suggested that it generated close to nine dinars of additional exports for one dinar of matching grant. The problem, though, is that of size and scale. In Tunisia and elsewhere, such interventions tend to focus on small and medium enterprises (SMEs), often considered as prime job creators. As a matter of fact, firm-level evidence suggests that young age rather than small size is associated with job creation; out of many small firms, only a few young ones will grow and create jobs on a significant scale. Moreover, small firms only make up for a tiny share of aggregate exports. Thus, although export promotion programs may appear to work, they cannot be game-changers.

Taken together, the findings in the report suggest that the success of MENA countries to promote export growth and diversification as well as create jobs depends heavily on their ability to create an environment where large firms can invest and expand exports and new efficient firms can thrive to the top.

A number of policy options are likely to help achieve this objective:

1. Governments in MENA should seek a competitive real exchange rate (RER) that will help firms grow and gain access to new markets. MENA exchange rate regimes are still predominantly pegged regimes. In a world where MENA exporters are faced with Chinese and other Asian price competitors, with currencies significantly undervalued against the dollar, the exchange rate cannot be ignored in a strategy to boost exporters' competitiveness. How could MENA countries move to more flexible exchange rate regimes? Until now, any exchange-rate adjustment was difficult to manage fiscally because of the prevalence of energy subsidies. Eliminating subsidies especially now that energy prices are at an historical low is a first step in adjusting the exchange rate to more competitive levels.

2. Governments in MENA need to make significant strides in improving the business climate to facilitate the entry of young, efficient firms and attract productive foreign companies. For this, governments need to significantly reduce trade costs, by improving the quality of infrastructure, improving trade logistics, and streamlining export procedures. Eliminating restrictions on the internal movement of labor and goods will also help raise firms' productivity and hence competitiveness. Governments also need to push trade reforms more energetically. Closing MENA markets to competition with high tariffs and restrictive non-tariff measures (NTMs) has not helped domestic exporters grow. The region's governments need to facilitate efficient sourcing of inputs by eliminating high-tariffs on intermediate imports to help domestic firms'

Champions Wanted • http://dx.doi.org/10.1596/978-1-4648-0460-1

participate in GVC. Modernizing domestic NTMs will also help firms over-come managerial failures and encourage companies to innovate. Publicizing the domestic enforcement of high norms as a quality-signaling strategy may also help expand the constituency in favor of more regulatory convergence.

3. Attracting foreign direct investment (FDI) has particular importance in the development of effective export champions. Superstars typically enter the export market when they are relatively large, often through foreign invest-ment, and reach the top 1 percent within a few years of exporting. This high-lights the role of multinationals in exports. Furthermore, the entry of new large exporters will expand competitive pressure on incumbents and boost overall performance. In MENA, the weaker performance and life-cycle dynamics of the top 1 percent could reflect lower levels of competition from foreign companies resulting from lower flows of FDI going to the region. Thus, policies to attract large, productive multinational firms are likely to be crucial for MENA countries' exports and diversification. As foreign compa-nies tend to pay higher wages, FDI would contribute to the job agenda too. Importantly, given the region's track record, there is a very real concern that attempts to facilitate the emergence of export champions may be captured and tailored to a few, favored firms rather than enable the entry or growth of young productive ones.

4. Finally, if the goal is to increase exports and diversification, MENA governments may need to rethink their approach to export promotion. The fact that very few large firms make up the bulk of exports implies that entry costs are rela-tively less important than variable trade costs for promoting aggregate exports. Policies that disproportionately allocate resources to help SMEs enter the export market, by lowering entry costs or offering subsidized resources, are unlikely, even if they work, to translate into economically meaningful aggre-gate effects—since these firms are too small to make a big difference. Only if SMEs in MENA are small because of distortions that prevent them from grow-ing to be large firms, could policies that help eliminate such distortions have important aggregate effects. But their focus needs to be on removing distor-tions not promoting specific firms.

Many of these policy recommendations are the types of reforms that develop-ment institutions, such as the World Bank, have been advising countries in MENA to implement over the past decade. The difference this time is that the firm-level evidence in this report allows MENA governments to better quantify the costs, in terms of forgone trade and jobs, of not having moved ahead more rapidly on such reforms.

References

Porter, Michael. 1991. "America's Green Strategy." *Scientific American* 264 (4): 168.

Porter, M., and C. van der Linde. 1995. "Toward a New Conception of the Environment-Competitiveness Relationship." *Journal of Economic Perspectives* 9 (4): 97–118.

Abbreviations

AVE	ad valorem equivalent
BEC	broad economic categories
CEEC	Central and East European Coalition
DC	developing countries
EDD	Exporter Dynamics Database
EPA	export-promotion agency
EU	European Union
FDI	foreign direct investment
FOB	free-on-board
GDP	gross domestic product
GDPPC	gross domestic product per capita
GVC	global value chains
HS	harmonized system
INS	Institut National de la Statistique
JEDCO	Jordan Enterprise Development Corporation
LAC	Latin American countries
MAST	multi-agency support team
MENA	Middle East and North Africa
MFN	most favored nation
MRI	Mobility Restriction Index
NTM	non-tariff measure
OAMDI	Open Access Micro Data Initiative
OECD	Organisation for Economic Co-operation and Development
PTM	pricing-to-market
RCA	revealed comparative advantage
RD	regulatory distance
RER	real exchange rate

SME	small and medium enterprise
SPS	sanitary and phytosanitary (standards)
TBT	technical barriers to trade
UNCTAD	United Nations Conference on Trade and Development
U.S.	United States
WTO	World Trade Organization

CHAPTER 1

Introduction

Exports for Growth, More and Better Jobs

The political events reshaping the Middle East and North Africa (MENA) have highlighted the urgency of creating jobs, raising the return to education, and distributing the benefits of growth more widely. Export-led growth can deliver all three. A large trade literature shows that exporting firms are larger, more productive, less financially constrained, and more skill and capital-intensive than their domestic counterparts (Melitz 2003; Bernard and Jensen 2004; Eaton, Kortum, and Kramarz 2004; Chaney 2013). Most relevant to the job challenges in MENA countries, exporters also create more jobs, pay higher wages and offer better working conditions than firms involved in domestic production (Bernard and Jensen 1995; Brambilla, Lederman, and Porto 2012; Frías, Kaplan, and Verhoogen 2012). Consistent with the literature, box 1.1 confirms the positive impact of international trade participation for job reaction in the case of Tunisia. However, MENA as a whole has lagged significantly in trade with the rest of the world and as a result in the creation of more and better jobs.

Firm-Level Perspectives on MENA Trade Performance

The standard narrative that MENA under-trades, is closed and fragmented, has failed to push reforms sufficiently hard, and suffers from widespread corruption and cronyism is well documented at the aggregate level (see World Bank 2009, 2014). However, little is known about firm-level exporter behavior largely because of a lack of data. The purpose of this report is to fill this knowledge gap. Using new firm-level export data, collected in eight MENA countries— the Arab Republic of Egypt, the Islamic Republic of Iran, Jordan, Kuwait, Lebanon, Morocco, Tunisia and the Republic of Yemen—we provide a micro-perspective on why the MENA region under-exports. The focus of the report is therefore on exporting firms in MENA.

Four main findings emerge from this report. First, the size distribution of MENA's exporting firms is suggestive of a critical weakness at the top. MENA has champions (the individual firms at the top of the distributions) of a size

Box 1.1 Exports Matter for Jobs: Evidence from Tunisia

This box focuses on Tunisia, where the firm-level customs data was merged with the industrial firm census, and provides evidence of the employment creation premium associated
with participating in international trade. Figure B1.1.1 clearly shows that while trade participation is relatively rare—with only about 8.5 percent of all Tunisian firms exporting and
16.5 percent of them importing—firms that participate in international trade account for a
very significant share of wage employment. Exporters account for more than a third of all
wage jobs, importers for more than half, and firms that export and/or import account for
over 55 percent of total wage jobs.

   The tax regime under which firms operate also matters. Offshore firms, whose activities are
predominantly focused on exporting, represent only 6 percent of all firms that offer wage jobs,
but accounted for roughly 33 percent of wage employment in 2010 (table B1.1.1). Moreover,
approximately 45 percent of offshore firms are foreign-owned. This reflects the success of
export processing zones in attracting foreign companies to Tunisia. Such foreign firms
contribute a significant share of job creation. In 2010, foreign-owned firms operating under an
offshore status accounted for over 16 percent of wage jobs while they only accounted for
roughly 3 percent of firms that offer wage jobs.

   In terms of net job creation, table B1.1.2 suggests that offshore firms create more jobs in net
than onshore firms. However, this is due to offshore firms being larger, younger, engaged in
trading activities, and foreign owned. In fact, while the coefficient on the offshore dummy is

Figure B1.1.1 Trade Participation and Employment

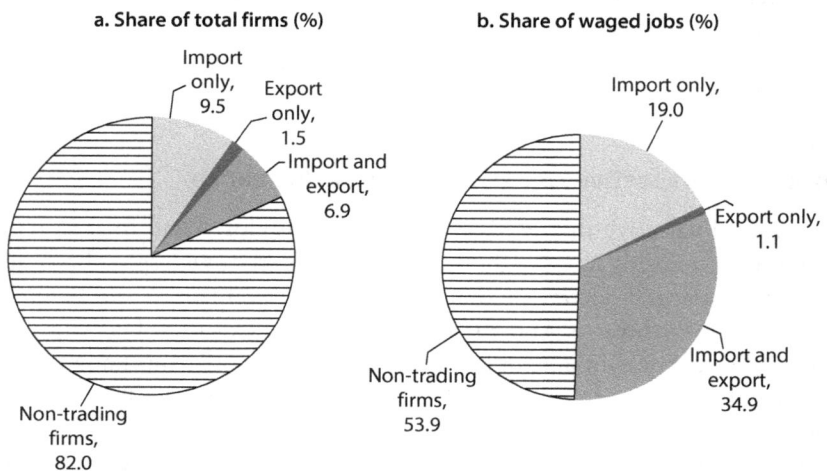

a. Share of total firms (%)

Import only, 9.5
Export only, 1.5
Import and export, 6.9
Non-trading firms, 82.0

b. Share of waged jobs (%)

Import only, 19.0
Export only, 1.1
Import and export, 34.9
Non-trading firms, 53.9

Source: Calculation based on Rijkers et al. 2014.
Note: We consider firms with more than one person, to allow for a comparison of the share of trading firms
in total number of firms (panel a) and in total number of wage jobs (panel b), since wage jobs exclude
self-employment. Data are for the year 2010.

box continues next page

Box 1.1 Exports Matter for Jobs: Evidence from Tunisia *(continued)*

Table B1.1.1 Employment, Trade, and Tax Regime

	Number of firms	*Number of wage jobs*	*Percent of all wage jobs*
All	597,597	982,986	
Exporter	6,420	360,264	36.65
Offshore	19,211	319,457	32.50
Exporter and offshore	3,325	223,873	22.77
Foreign	10,946	180,732	18.39
Foreign and offshore	8,261	166,151	16.90

Source: Rijkers et al. 2014.
Note: Here we report all firms including one-person firms. Wage jobs do not account for self-employment, and thus exclude the contribution of single-person firms. All numbers are for 2010, which is the last year with available data.

Table B1.1.2 Net Job Creation and International Orientation

	(1)	*(2)*	*(3)*	*(4)*	*(5)*	*(6)*
Offshore	0.074	0.021	−0.054	−0.05	−0.095	−0.055
Foreign		0.115	0.046	0.052	0.046	0.046
Exporting				0.046	0.006	−0.042
Importing					0.091	0.08
Exporting & importing						0.053
Firm size dummies	No	No	Yes	Yes	Yes	Yes
Firm age dummies	No	No	Yes	Yes	Yes	Yes
Year dummies	Yes	Yes	Yes	Yes	Yes	Yes
Activity dummies	Yes	Yes	Yes	Yes	Yes	Yes

Source: Rijkers et al. 2014.
Note: The dependent variable is the Davis-Haltiwanger-Schuh growth rate, which allows for an integrated treatment of the contributions of entering, continuing, and exiting firms. The regressions are weighted and control for industry and year effects; the resulting coefficients are thus interpretable as conditional average net job flows. All coefficients are significant at the 1 percent level; therefore, we do not report significance level. Data are for the year 2010.

positive and significant in the first column without controlling for firm size, trade orientation, and ownership, it becomes negative and significant once these characteristics are accounted for (column 6).

Importantly, the last column in table B1.1.2 suggests that the job creation differences between firms that participate in international trade and those that do not are in large part driven by firms that both import and export, which exhibit the largest performance difference from domestic firms. The coefficient on the interaction term in the last column suggests that firms that both import and export create jobs on average 5.3 percent faster. Foreign companies create jobs 4.6 percentage points faster than the average domestic non-trading firm, suggesting that foreign direct investment plays a key role in advancing both exports and job creation in the host country.

Interestingly, importing-only firms appear to be performing extremely well. As will be discussed in the last chapter of the report, politically connected firms under the Ben Ali regime benefited from privileged access to import licenses. This may be suggestive

box continues next page

Box 1.1 Exports Matter for Jobs: Evidence from Tunisia *(continued)*

evidence that political favors tend to come with reciprocating obligations in the form of over-hiring.

While these results are obtained in the case of Tunisia they align with previous findings in the trade literature and have implications for all the MENA countries. Taken together they suggest that in MENA as elsewhere, policies that will help develop effective export champions will help create more and better jobs in the process. Providing them with the right enabling environment is the region's key policy challenge.

Source: Based on Rijkers et al. 2014.

comparable to other regions, but it lacks teams of world-class exporters to surround and emulate the number ones, its top 1 percent exporters being significantly smaller, on average, than in other regions. Thus, MENA countries have failed to nurture a group of export champions which critically contribute to export growth and diversification in other regions. Small size also means that MENA's champions do not punch as heavy as they should. We find that MENA exporters lack market power on their destination markets compared to a control group of exporters from other developing or emerging regions. It may also be a consequence of insufficient innovation and drive. Top exporters in MENA do not seem to drive comparative advantage at the country level as is typically found in other regions. On one hand these results suggest that MENA superstars may lack the right environment and incentives to thrive. On the other hand it may suggest that large-firm strategies reflect, at least partly, a legacy of distorted incentives.

Second, the firm-level and the aggregate evidence confirm exchange-rate policy as a priority area for policy action. At the aggregate level we re-examines the extent of the MENA region's under-trading and find that region-wide aggregates hide considerable heterogeneity, and many elements of the standard narrative, while true for the region's unreformed resource-rich countries, do not hold for the resource-poor ones, including the "MENA-4"—Egypt, Jordan, Morocco, and Tunisia. The MENA-4 under-trading is a mixture of under-exporting and over-importing suggestive of macroeconomic distortions, such as real-exchange rate overvaluation. At the firm-level, recent literature provides a wealth of evidence on the inhibiting effects of overvalued currencies on firm-level expansion of trade volumes and introduction of new product into new markets, with insights directly applicable to MENA.

Third, the new firm-level evidence suggests that the success of MENA countries to promote export growth and diversification as well as create jobs depends heavily on their ability to create an environment that will allow existing dynamic and large firms to grow while facilitating the entry of young, efficient firms and FDI at a large scale. Encouraging the entry of new additional large exporters will also expand competitive pressure on incumbents and boost overall performance. The report provides strong, firm-level evidence that export performance correlates with the quality of imported intermediaries, suggesting that the region's governments should break from their traditional logic "export, do not import" to a policy of facilitation of efficient sourcing. As users of imported inputs tend to be larger, more efficient exporters, facilitating access to higher quality or cheaper inputs is also likely to achieve better results. The report also highlights the role that regulatory modernization can play in enhancing firm competitiveness. Contrary to widely-held views, more stringent regulations do not necessarily hurt the competitiveness of domestic firms. They can have a clean-up effect on the domestic market by keeping out lower-end suppliers, providing better incentives to upgrade quality. They can also (this is the "Porter hypothesis") help overcome managerial failures and encourage companies to innovate (Porter 1991; Porter and van der Linde 1995).

Fourth, in MENA as elsewhere, sluggish export performance makes it tempting for governments to resort to industrial policy, in spite of the negative record of State intervention in the region. MENA's prevalent cronyism and corruption under pre-Arab Spring regimes confirms that business-government ties led to distortionary allocation of favors and rent dissipation by beneficiary firms, with little evidence that those firms developed into national champions or helped lift the region's export performance. This in itself should call for caution when advocating any form of government intervention. Yet, while the potential for capture and government failures is large, some intervention, like export promotion, seem to work. For instance, a recent impact evaluation of Tunisia's FAMEX program suggested that it generated close to nine dinars of additional exports for one dinar of matching grant, although the effects on firms were short-lived. The problem is more one of size and impact. Such interventions tend to focus on SMEs, as those firms are often considered as prime job creators. Yet, the firm-level evidence suggests that young age rather than smallness imply job creation; out of many small firms, only a few young ones will grow and create jobs on a significant scale. Moreover, small firms contribute little to aggregate export performance. Thus, although export promotion programs may appear to work, they cannot be game changers. These results suggest that in MENA as elsewhere, if the quest is to achieve higher levels of export development and diversification, governments may need to rethink their approach to export promotion.

The rest of the report proceeds as follows. Chapter 2 characterizes exporting firms in MENA and brings a new perspective to our understanding of MENA's weak aggregate export performance. Chapter 3 examines how the lack of a competitive exchange rate has had deleterious effects all the way down to the level of the firm. Chapter 4 examines how MENA's lagging trade and business climate reforms have contributed to the region's failure to develop effective export champions and how this in turn has potentially high costs in terms of exports and jobs. Chapter 5 discusses how the new firm-level evidence can help better assess the legacy and prospects of policy interventions across the region. Finally, the report concludes by discussing several policy options that may help MENA countries create the right enabling environment where large firms can invest and expand exports and new efficient firms can thrive to the top.

Champions Wanted • http://dx.doi.org/10.1596/978-1-4648-0460-1

References

Bernard, A., and B. Jensen. 1995. "Exporters, Jobs and Wages in U.S. Manufacturing, 1976–87." *Brookings Papers on Economic Activity: Microeconomics* 1995: 67–112.

———. 2004. "Why Some Firms Export." *Review of Economics and Statistics* 86: 561–69.

Brambilla, I., D. Lederman, and G. Porto. 2012. "Exports, Export Destinations, and Skills." *American Economic Review* 102: 3406–38.

Chaney, Thomas. 2013. "Liquidity Constrained Exporters." NBER Working Paper 19170, National Bureau of Economic Research, Boston, MA.

Eaton, J., S. Kortum, and F. Kramarz. 2004. "Dissecting Trade: Firms, Industries, and Export Destinations." *American Economic Review* 94: 150–54.

———. 2011. "An Anatomy of International Trade: Evidence from French Firms." *Econometrica* 79: 1453–98.

Frías, J., D. Kaplan, and E. Verhoogen. 2012. "Exports and Wage Premia: Evidence from Mexican Employer-Employee Data." *American Economic Review Papers & Proceedings* 102: 435–40.

Manova, Kalina. 2011. "Credit Constraints, Heterogeneous Firms, and International Trade." *Review of Economic Studies* 80: 711–44.

Melitz, Marc J. 2003. "The Impact of Trade on Intra-Industry Reallocations and Aggregate Industry Productivity." *Econometrica* 71: 1695–725.

Porter, Michael. 1991. "America's Green Strategy." *Scientific American* 264 (4): 168.

Porter, M., and C. van der Linde. 1995. "Toward a New Conception of the Environment-Competitiveness Relationship." *Journal of Economic Perspectives* 9 (4): 97–118.

Rijkers, B., A. Arouri, C. Freund, and A. Nucifora. 2014. "Which Firms Create the most jobs in developing countries? Evidence from Tunisia." Policy Research Working Paper Series 7068, World Bank.

Verhoogen, Eric. 2008. "Trade, Quality Upgrading, and Wage Inequality in the Mexican Manufacturing Sector." *Quarterly Journal of Economics* 123 (2): 489–530.

Wagner, Joachim. 2012. "International Trade and Firm Performance: A Survey of Empirical Studies since 2006." *Review of World Economics* 148: 235–67.

World Bank. 2009. *From Privilege to Competition: Unlocking Private-Led Growth in the Middle East and North Africa*. Washington, DC: World Bank.

———. 2014. *Jobs or Privileges: Unleashing the Employment Potential of the Middle East and North Africa*. Washington, DC: World Bank.

CHAPTER 2

One Champion, but No Team

Key Messages

While other emerging regions were thriving, the Middle East and North Africa's (MENA) aggregate export performance over the past two decades has been consistently weak. There is no dearth of candidate explanations at the macro level, including (inter alia) poor governance and macroeconomic fundamentals, political instability, and high trade costs. Using detailed firm-level export data from Customs administrations, this chapter sheds new light on the issue at the micro level. We show that with the exception of the top firm, MENA's elite exporters—the top 1 percent, which accounts for more than half of exports and export growth—are smaller and weaker compared to their peers in other regions. Thus, in MENA the largest exporter is alone at the top—Zidane without a team.

Who Are MENA Exporters?

Traditionally, MENA's weak trade performance has been discussed at the aggregate level in terms of countries and sectors. The entire MENA region, with a population close to 320 million, has fewer nonoil exports than Finland or Hungary (as noted in Nabli et al. 2006). In addition, despite evidence of convergence over the past decade, with MENA's exports expanding more rapidly than exports from the rest of the world, it would take 20 years for MENA countries to reach their potential trade (Behar and Freund 2011). The region's undertrading is compounded by its inability to trade with itself, as political fragmentation limits effective regional integration in the Arab world (Rouis and Tabor 2013).[1] A number of studies have also pointed to the very limited supply response of MENA's many trade agreements. While partners outside MENA tend to increase exports to the region subsequent to a trade agreement, MENA exports remain stagnant (see Nugent 2002; Cieslik and Hagemejer 2009; Freund and Portugal 2013).[2]

Yet, countries do not trade; firms do. Aggregate data hide a lot of heterogeneity and do not allow us to distinguish which firms drive aggregate export volumes, growth, and diversification, nor which margins of adjustments matter most. Using detailed firm-level export data from Customs administrations gathered for the use of the report and part of the larger World Bank Exporter Dynamics Database, we study the characteristics and dynamics of MENA exporters themselves to understand MENA countries' lagging export performance. Appendix A describes in details the firm-level customs data and provides definitions of the variables used.

While our focus is on MENA countries, the analysis presented makes use of the complete dataset to benchmark the region against the rest of the world. Except for Kuwait, the Islamic Republic of Iran and, to some extent the Republic of Yemen, countries in the sample are resource-poor and labor-abundant; thus, most of the analysis and policy implications are focused on them, leaving aside issues related to natural resources and diversification (see Diop, Marotta, and de Melo 2012 for recent work on this issue).

Figure 2.1 illustrates how exporters in MENA differ from exporters in other developing countries in terms of their characteristics and size. Once the size, income level, and sectoral differences across countries are accounted for, MENA as a whole, appears to have significantly fewer exporters, −26 percent less, than non-MENA countries. The annual export value per firm in MENA is US$1.02 million on average over the period 2006–08, less than half that of firms in other regions (see table 2.1). Considering countries individually, all but Lebanon are below the benchmark, although in the case of Morocco and the Islamic Republic of Iran, the differences are not statistically significant, placing them exactly with countries at similar stages of development (figure 2.1 panel a).

Looking at the size distribution of exporters, table 2.1 shows that within countries, there is a large difference between the median and the mean values per exporter. This illustrates one of the most striking features of trade data, namely that exports are concentrated in the hands of a few large firms (Bernard et al. 2007; Mayer and Ottaviano 2007; Freund and Pierola forthcoming). However, while the mean export values are, on average, 54 times larger than the median export values per exporter in non-MENA developing countries, this figure drops to 17 times in MENA, suggesting that the distribution of non-oil exports is relatively less skewed in MENA than elsewhere. This is further evidenced in figure 2.1 where MENA displays both smaller average exporters (panel b) and larger median exporters (panel c), than elsewhere.

The lack of mass at the top of the distribution is also confirmed when considering the share of exports accounted for by the top 5 percent largest exporters. In non-MENA countries the top 5 percent account for over 80 percent of total non-oil exports on average, against 76 percent in a typical MENA country. Taken individually, MENA countries all exhibit less depth in the top 5 percent largest exporters, although again the difference is not statistically significant for Morocco (panel d).

In terms of diversification patterns, table 2.1 suggests that exporters in MENA are roughly comparable to exporters in other developing countries, exporting about 4 products (defined at the HS 4-digit level) to just above 2 destination

Figure 2.1 Who Are MENA Exporters?

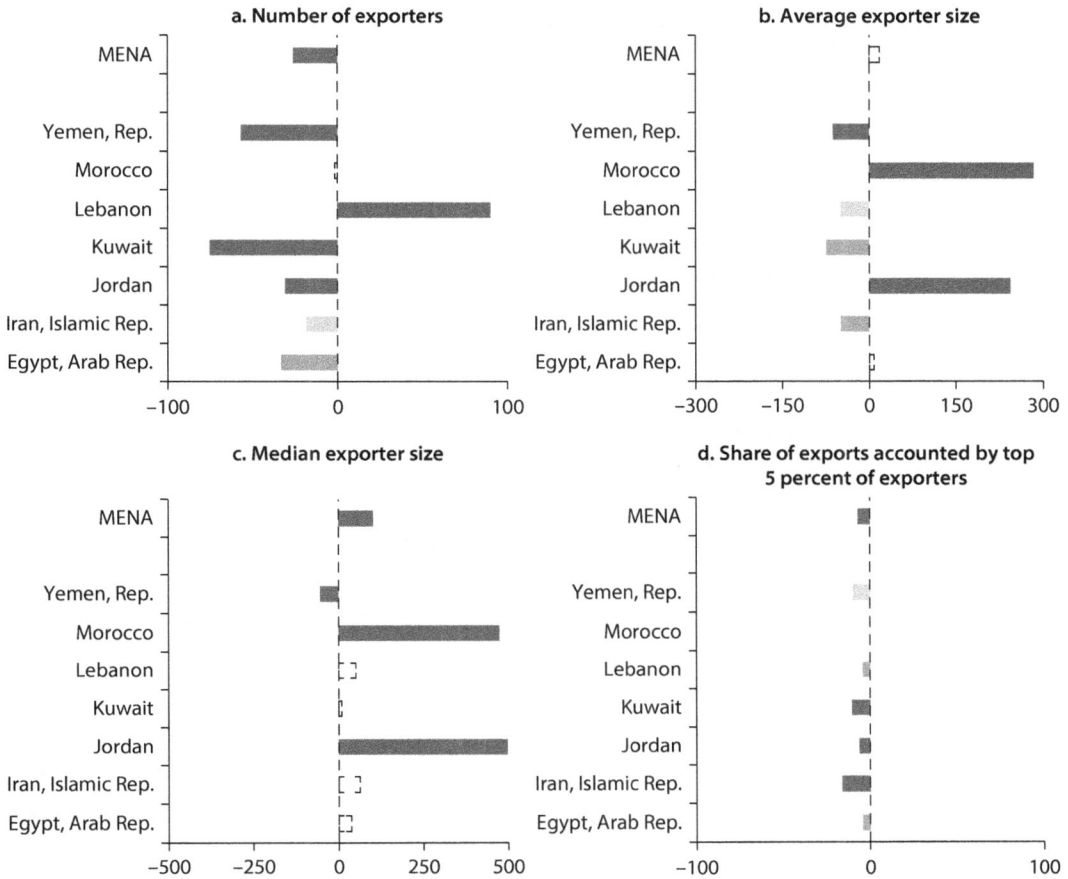

Source: Fernandes 2014.
Note: Each graph reports the coefficients on regional and country dummies in cross-country panel regressions of key characteristics of the exporter competitiveness indicators on exporting-country GDP, GDP per capita, sector, and year fixed effects. For each indicator the length of the bar gives the deviation (in percent) of the MENA region and each MENA country individually from the rest of the world. Blue, orange, and green denote significance at 1, 5, and 10 percent, respectively. Insignificant estimates are shown as blank bars with dotted lines. The sample covers the 34 countries in the dataset with data at the country-HS 4-digit-year level in any or all years from 2006 until 2011. Tunisia and West Bank are not included in the dataset and thus regression results do not report dummies for those two economies.

markets in any given year (see table 2.1). Importantly, this average hides significant heterogeneity across firms. One reason why trade is so concentrated is that large exporters not only export more of a given product, they export more products to more destinations. In short, large exporters are also diversified exporters. Figure 2.2 reports the distribution of exporters and total export shares by the number of products and destinations served in MENA and other developing countries. Although this is a feature of all exporter distributions, the majority of exporters in MENA (30 percent) sell only one product to one destination while accounting for just over 1 percent of total exports. By contrast the

Table 2.1 Exporters in MENA: Summary Statistics

	MENA countries	Other developing countries
Firm-level		
Exports (millions of USD)		
Mean	1.02	2.18
Median	0.06	0.04
Standard deviation	15.71	52.13
Number of HS 4-digit products		
Mean	4.41	4.76
Median	2.00	2.00
Standard deviation	8.96	11.61
Number of destinations		
Mean	2.15	2.34
Median	1.00	1.00
Standard deviation	2.96	3.44
Aggregate-level		
Number of firms	54,783	260,106
Number of HS 4-digit products	1,201	1,223
Number of destinations	195	218
Exports (millions of USD)	137,888	1,528,503

Source: Brunel, Fernandes, and Jaud 2015.
Note: The figures are computed as averages for the 2006–08 period, based on firm-level customs data for 34 countries.

Figure 2.2 Distribution of Firms and Export Values by Product-Destination Coverage

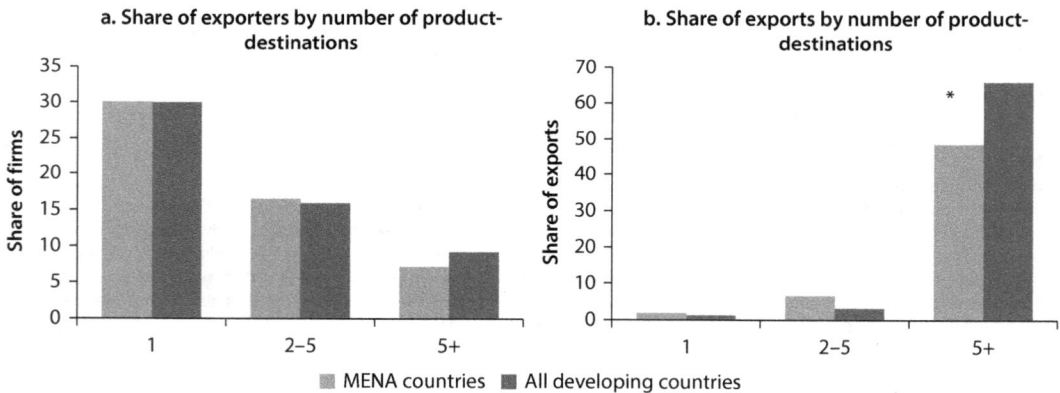

a. Share of exporters by number of product-destinations

b. Share of exports by number of product-destinations

■ MENA countries ■ All developing countries

Source: Brunel, Fernandes, and Jaud 2015.
Note: Products are defined at the HS 4-digit level. Data in both panels show averages for the 2006–08 period, based on firm-level customs data for 34 countries. The category labelled "1" indicates that the firm exports 1 product to 1 destination, that labelled "2–5" indicates that the firm exports 2–5 products and to 2–5 destinations, and that labelled "5+" indicates that the firm exports more than 5 products and to more than 5 destinations. The asterisk marks significances at the 1 percent level.

proportion of diversified exporters—firms exporting at least 5 products to at least 5 destinations—is lower than elsewhere and accounts for a significantly lower share of total exports, 13 percent less, in MENA compared to the developing countries' average. This again points to weakness at the top of the distribution for MENA exporters. Within firms—even for those diversified

Figure 2.3 How Diversified Are MENA Exporters?

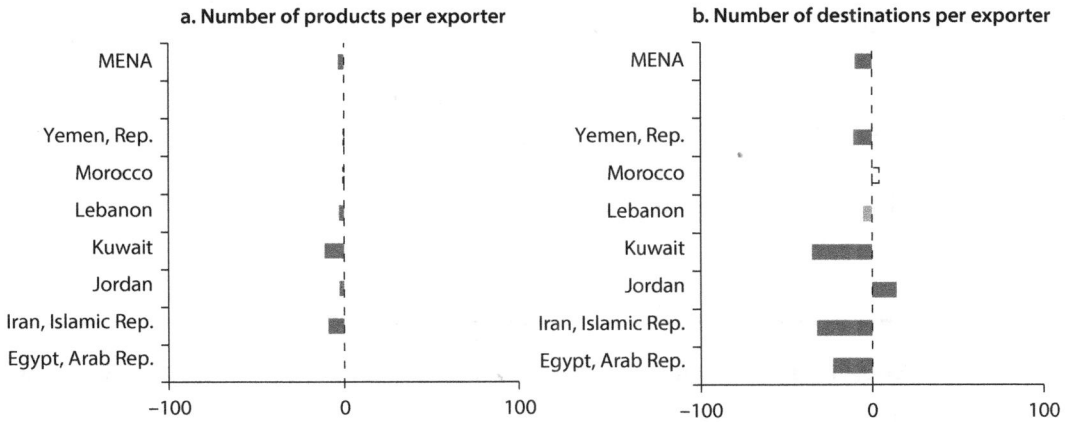

a. Number of products per exporter

b. Number of destinations per exporter

Source: Fernandes 2014.
Note: Each graph reports the coefficients on regional and country dummies in cross-country panel regressions of key characteristics of the exporter competitiveness indicators on exporting-country GDP, GDP per capita, sector, and year fixed effects. For each indicator the length of the bar gives the deviation (in percent) of the MENA region and each MENA country individually from the rest of the world. Blue, orange, and green denote significance at 1, 5, and 10 percent, respectively. Insignificant estimates are shown as blank bars with dotted lines. The sample covers the 34 countries in the dataset with data at the country-HS 4-digit-year level in any or all years from 2006 until 2011. Tunisia and West Bank are not included in the dataset and thus regression results do not report dummies for those two economies.

exporters—concentration is high, with over 40 percent of exports concentrated in the best performing product or destination. This may partly reflect their proximity to the large EU market, and the fact that MENA firms specialize in a different mix of products. MENA exporters indeed specialize significantly more in exports of primary products, commodities, and low-technology manufactures than exporters in other developing countries.

Figure 2.3 confirms that exporters in MENA are only slightly less diversified both in terms of their products (–3 percent) and their destination markets (–10 percent) than the average exporter elsewhere. Product-wise except for the major oil exporting countries—the Islamic Republic of Iran and Kuwait, for which product under-diversification is to be expected—the rest of MENA countries exhibit a standard level of diversification. In terms of geographic concentration, the regional average hides substantial heterogeneity across individual MENA countries. Again oil exporting countries, the Islamic Republic of Iran, Kuwait, and the Republic of Yemen, exhibit significantly higher geographic concentrations, while Jordan's firms export to a significantly higher number of destinations, and Morocco and Lebanon are mostly in line with countries at their stage of development.

If anything, product-diversification is not that much of an issue at the firm-level. As to geographic concentration, given MENA countries' proximity to the EU it is somewhat to be expected. The issue is rather that of the associated vulnerability to destination–specific shocks. The over-concentration of exports on EU markets—particularly southern ones—has indeed exposed countries like Morocco and Tunisia to the recession in those markets. In addition, evidence at the firm-level confirms that destination diversification helps survival at the product level. Even when they are diversified destination-wise firms in MENA still exhibit lower probabilities of export survival compared to firms in other regions, reflecting their smaller size.[3] The Islamic Republic of Iran, which suffered severe trade sanctions by its main trading partner, offers an opportunity to examine the role of geographic diversification on firms' ability to absorb destination-specific shocks and survive on export markets (see box 2.1).

Box 2.1 Sanctions and Trade Deflection: Evidence from the Islamic Republic of Iran

The Islamic Republic of Iran has recently suffered important trade-related sanctions from major trading partners—including the United States, the United Kingdom, European Union member states, Canada, and Australia. This box builds on Haidar (2014) and evaluates the impact of trade sanctions, which are equivalent to destination-specific trade shocks, on firms' export decisions.

While sanctions reduced Iranian firms' exports to sanction-imposing destinations—by roughly a third—overall Iranian exports did not decrease, suggesting that firms redeployed to alternative sanctions-free markets. Figure B2.1.1 illustrates this dynamic. Over the 2006–11 period, the evolution of the entry and exit rates of Iranian firms' exports in sanctions-imposing and sanction-free markets are almost mirror images. This re-deployment compensated up to two-thirds of the loss incurred due to sanctions.

Figure B2.1.1 Exporters' Dynamics with or without Sanctions

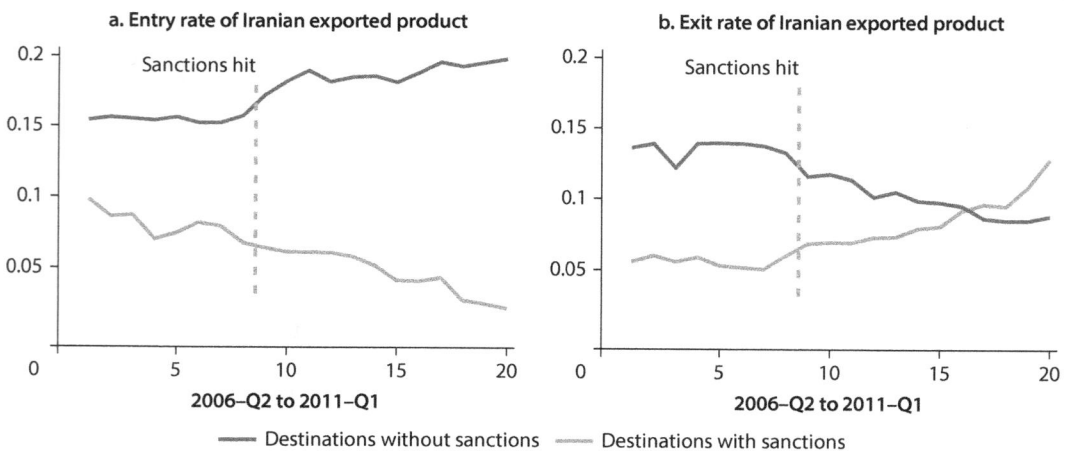

a. Entry rate of Iranian exported product

b. Exit rate of Iranian exported product

—— Destinations without sanctions   —— Destinations with sanctions

Source: Haidar 2014.
Note: Entry and exit rates are computed at the firm-product-destination-level and averaged across destinations with and without sanctions, from the second quarter of 2006 to first quarter of 2011.

box continues next page

Box 2.1 Sanctions and Trade Deflection: Evidence from the Islamic Republic of Iran *(continued)*

The choice of destinations, however, was not random. Exporters mainly redirected exports towards destinations they had previous experience with, taking advantage of networks and information previously gained on those markets. Small exporters were hit the hardest, which is consistent with the idea that sanctions act as a tax on exports, and that larger, less financially-constrained exporters are better able to bear these additional costs. Finally, exporting firms successfully penetrated new markets with their core products, suggesting that following sanctions, firms' profitability decreased, forcing them to concentrate on their most profitable core products.

These findings provide evidence that sanctions may be less effective in a globalized world, as firms can divert their trade from one trading partner to another. The results also highlight the importance of diversification in terms of destinations, allowing exporters to weather the impact of potential destination-level shocks.

Source: Haidar 2014.

Interestingly, because firms are heterogeneous in their ability to absorb shocks—with smaller and less productive firms being hit the hardest and being the first to exit the export market—overall the effect of sanctions are likely to be limited as ultimately these firms account for a small share of total exports.

Beyond this static characterization of exporters' diversification, what matters is how the diversification process takes place and whether MENA firms differ from their counterpart in the rest of the world in this respect. In terms of dynamics, exporters in MENA mostly resemble exporters in other developing countries, whereby they typically begin exporting a single product to a single foreign market—mostly neighboring countries defined as geographically close countries and former colonizers—and, if they survive, gradually expand into additional destinations, again mostly neighboring countries.

Alone at the Top

Over 2006–08, MENA had on average 34,450 exporters; however, the largest 344 of these firms accounted for the bulk, 52 percent, of its total exports. This highly skewed distribution of exporters in MENA that is also verified around the world implies that a very small group of firms are disproportionately shaping exports. In this section, we thus focus on the top 1 percent largest exporters, the so-called export superstars, and examine their role in explaining MENA weak export performance.

Figure 2.4 plots the log of each firm's rank in the size distribution against the log of its size (export value), averaged over 30 countries in the sample for the year 2008. Given the log-log scale, the almost linear relationship shown in panel (a) implies a "power law" characterized by heavy concentration of

Figure 2.4 The Top Firm Is Unique in MENA

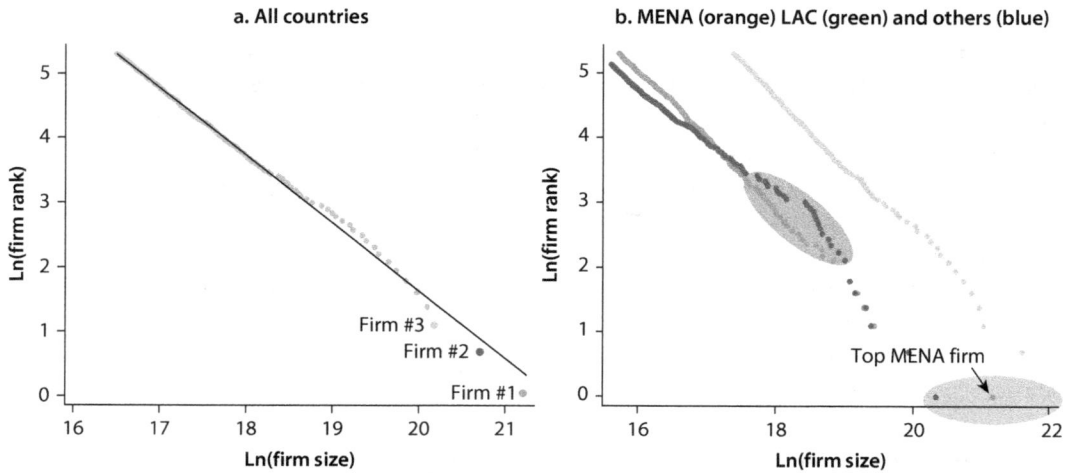

Source: Freund and Pierola 2014.
Note: The data are from 2008 and cover 30 developing countries. Each point is a firm. The vertical axis starts at ln(1) = 0 for the firm ranked first in the size distribution, which is the dot at the extreme Southeast corner of the plot. Moving Northwest, the next dot is the firm ranked second, and so on. In panel (a), sizes are averaged at each rank across all countries in the sample. Thus, the average size of the largest firm, across all countries, is slightly above exp(21), which is about US$1.4 billion. In panel (b), separate distributions are plotted for three groups of countries: MENA (orange), LAC (green), and others (blue). The orange-shaded area marks the top firm for the three country groups.

exports among a few large firms. That is, when ranking exporters within each country from the best to the worst, the first firm exports twice as much as the second, three times as much as the third, and so on. This pattern holds for all countries. Panel (b) compares the same relationship for the average MENA country with other countries. There is one notable feature in the MENA distribution. While the top firm looks similar in terms of size to the average top firm in non-MENA or Latin American countries (LAC) (the orange-shaded zone), the distribution near the top (the blue-shaded zone) is a leftward shift of the distribution for other countries and even more of the distribution for LAC. While the shift relative to the "others" distribution appears small in the figure, given the log scale, it is substantial. Thus, the top firm in MENA is unique, and thus missing the many challengers that surround it in other regions.

To illustrate the importance of the group of export superstars, table 2.2 reports some summary statistics on superstars and non-superstars using aver-aged data from 2006 to 2008 for non-oil exports. The number of superstars varies substantially across countries depending on the size of the country and therefore the size of its export base. In MENA the median country has 52 superstars, against 27 for the median non-MENA country, although the vari-ation in this group is much larger (column 1). Despite being a relatively small number of firms, in MENA as in other developing countries, the top 1 percent

Table 2.2 Superstars' Characteristics

	SS = Top 1 percent of exporters				Top one exporter		
	Number of SS	Size relative to median non-SS	Share of non-oil exports (%)	Share of manufacturing exports (%)	Size relative to median non-SS	Share of non-oil exports (%)	Share of manufacturing exports (%)
	(1)	(2)	(3)	(4)	(5)	(6)	(7)
MENA							
Average	52	572	52	52	9,540	14	18
SD	46	262	7	6	8,243	6	8
Egypt, Arab Rep.	79	742	49	52	7,900	5	7
Iran, Islamic Rep.	135	175	53	59	23,416	16	21
Jordan	22	908	55	53	11,179	19	20
Lebanon	52	586	55	52	4,659	5	6
Morocco	51	558	51	49	16,893	13	16
Yemen, Rep.	5	358	37	42	943	15	24
Non-MENA							
Average	27	1,349	54	51	7,808	11	12
SD	74	1,145	18	19	67,396	15	15

Source: Freund and Pierola 2014.
Note: Statistics on total values exported, average firm size, firm number, for each country-year are averaged over the period 2006–08, and cover 30 developing countries. Manufacturing exports are defined according to the ISIC Classification Revision 3 (Chapters 15–37); SD = standard deviation.

represent over 50 percent of exports, whether all or manufacturing only (columns 3 and 4). Considering the "median superstar"—i.e., the median exporter size in the top 1 percent—in MENA it is only 500 times the size of the median non-superstar firm—i.e., the median exporter size in the remaining 99 percent—compared to about 1,000 times elsewhere. Therefore, relative to other developing countries, MENA's superstars are half as large.

In contrast, when we examine the top firm itself, the pattern is not significantly different in MENA from the rest of world. In a typical MENA country, the top exporter holds almost 15 percent of non-oil exports against 11 percent elsewhere (column 6); and is somewhat larger relative to the median non-superstar exporter than in all countries, although there is much more variation in the latter group (column 5). These results confirm the preliminary evidence in figure 2.4 that in MENA the top firm is relatively larger as compared with other regions.

In addition to driving export volumes, export superstars also account for about half of countries' total export growth at both the intensive margin (volume increases on existing product-destination cells) and the extensive margins (new products or destinations) in MENA and elsewhere. A big difference, however, is that in MENA, the top firm alone accounts for a third of aggregate export growth, against just 10 percent in other parts of the world. Excluding the frontrunner, the top 1 percent accounts for 45 percent of growth: less than in the rest of the world on average (48 percent) and far less than in LAC (58 percent).[4]

Lacking Market Power

The flip side of smallness is lack of market power. As data on market shares and domestic prices is not widely accessible, it has traditionally been difficult to assess market power at the firm-level. However, a recent and growing literature has established, both theoretically and empirically, that the extent of pricing to market (PTM) relates to firm size, efficiency and, ultimately, market power (see e.g. Feenstra, Gagnon, and Knetter 1996; Atkeson and Burstein 2008; Amiti, Itskhoki, and Konings 2014; Berman, Martin, and Mayer 2012; Auer and Schoenle 2013).[5]

PTM implies that firms react to shocks in the bilateral exchange-rate by adjusting their free-on-board (FOB) export price in the home currency, rather than by passing through shocks to consumer prices. To understand the intuition behind the interpretation of PTM as market power, consider the following example. Consider a subcontractor in a value chain with no market power at all—a t-shirt producer in Morocco selling to Walmart in the US, for example. If his home currency appreciates, he has no choice but to pass it on entirely to the consumer, as competition with other t-shirt producers already drives down profits to zero, leaving no room to cut margins. He may or may not lose market share as a result; but in terms of pricing he has no choice. If, however, his currency depreciates, the buyer "sees it through" and forces the price down by the full extent of the depreciation. Thus, either way, a price-taking producer has no choice but to pass through the entire currency shock. Any deviation from this behavior reveals market power. Based on this intuition, the price adjustment of exporters to exchange-rate variations, can serve as the identification mechanism to assess firms' market power in their destination markets.[6]

In our sample of twelve developing countries, including seven MENA counties, the average rate of PTM is around 10–15 percent (see figure 2.5). This is similar to estimates obtained for industrial countries.[7] That is, when faced with an exchange-rate shock, a typical exporter in the sample will alter his producer price in local currency by 10–15 percent of the shock and pass on the rest to consumer price. Importantly, for MENA exporters, the rate of PTM is about one-third lower, at 5.1 percent. This suggests that these exporters enjoy less market power in their export markets compared to a control group of exporters from other developing or emerging regions.

Being price takers is a consequence of MENA exporters being too small. This is also consistent with the lack of large exporters at the very top of the distribution presented in the previous section, as large firms tend to adjust more to exchange rate variations at the price margin. Small size means that MENA's champions do not punch as heavy as they should.

And Failing to Drive Comparative Advantage

MENA's missing teams of world-class exporters are also not leading the way in terms of comparative advantage. While in other countries, about 80 percent of the sectoral variation of exports is due to the presence of superstars, in MENA, the top

Figure 2.5 MENA Exporters Lack Punching Power

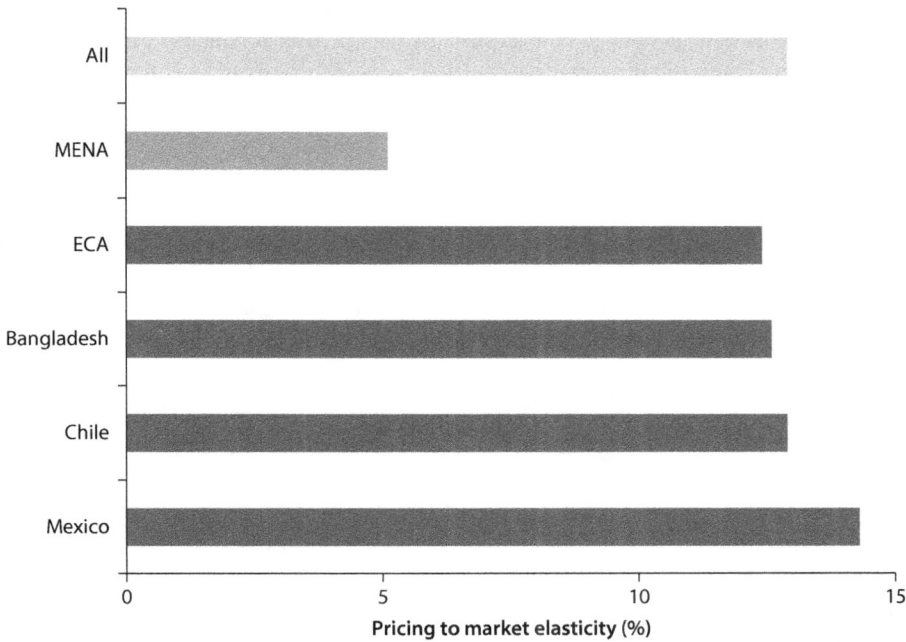

Source: Asprilla et al. 2014.
Note: The figure shows the results of regressions for different country groupings of the log of export unit values on the log of the real bilateral exchange rate, with firm-product-destination and origin-year fixed effects. The length of the bar reports the rate of PTM in percent, i.e., the exporter price elasticity to exchange rate, for each country or country group. The sample covers twelve low- and middle-income countries, including Bangladesh (2006–11), Chile (2004–09), Jordan (2004–11), Kenya (2006–11), Kuwait (2009–10), Lebanon (2009–10), Mexico (2001–09), Morocco (2003–11), Rwanda (2006–11), Tanzania (2006–11), Uganda (2005–11), and the Republic of Yemen (2007–11), with data at the firm-HS 8-destination-year level for different time period for each country.

1 percent explains only half of it, the same as their share in exports. Importantly, the pattern is reversed when looking at the top firm instead of the top 1 percent, with the top firm explaining a significantly larger share of variance than in other regions. These results are suggestive of a top firm that stands out in terms of its influence on MENA's trade patterns, while other MENA superstars contribute relatively less in terms of sectoral allocation than superstars in other countries.[8]

While superstars are responsible for such a large share of the variation in sectoral exports in much of the world, do they also drive comparative advantage? Considering all countries in the dataset, about 20 percent of revealed comparative advantage (RCA) industries owe their RCA status to the presence of superstars. These industries tend to be the larger sectors, as they account for about one-third of RCA trade.[9] Some clear patterns emerge, with industries that benefit from increasing returns to scale, such as chemicals, electrical machinery, metals, paper, and transport, driven by superstars; while superstars are not important for other industries, such as food, apparel, foodstuffs, glass, leather and wood (see appendix B). With respect to RCA, MENA as a region looks similar to other countries, with superstars accounting for 18 percent of comparative advantage sectors. However, when we compare to other middle income countries, MENA's performance is less remarkable. LAC shows the biggest role for superstars—with superstars accounting for nearly 30 percent of comparative advantage.

Figure 2.6 displays a scatter plot of stage of development and the share of RCA country-industries that would disappear if export superstars were removed from the data, for 38 countries. As countries get richer, exports become more concentrated, suggesting that the dominance of large firms is part of development (Freund and Pierola forthcoming). Perhaps, this is not too surprising if we consider that the biggest firms are the most productive. Channeling more resources to large firms increases output, which raises living standards. Interestingly, although there is important heterogeneity across countries, figure 2.6 suggests that this may also be true of the dominance of large firms in driving countries' comparative advantage. The graph shows a positive and significant correlation between countries' income level and the role of the top 1 percent in defining a country's comparative advantage. Middle-income countries, such as Mexico and South Africa, exhibit a greater reliance on superstars than poor countries, such as Uganda or the Republic of Yemen. In the Arab Republic of Egypt, Lebanon, Jordan, and the Republic of Yemen, superstars do not spearhead specialization as much as others developing at a similar stage of development. This is not the case in Morocco and the Islamic Republic of Iran.

These results highlight that while in all regions we find a skewed distribution of exporters, where the top 1 percent of exporters accounts for over 50 percent

Figure 2.6 Export Superstars and Revealed Comparative Advantage

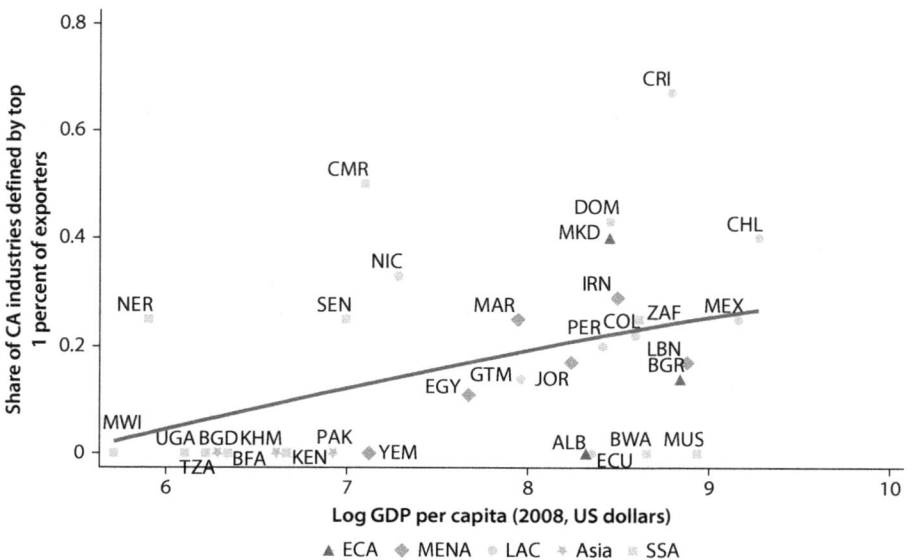

Source: Calculations based on Freund and Pierola 2014.
Note: The data are averaged over 2006–08 using 30 developing countries.

of exports, there are some notable distinctions between MENA and the rest of the world. The single largest firm in MENA tends to be relatively large as compared with other countries, while the other top firms are not as outstanding. In other words, MENA exporters are like a soccer team, with only one Zidane, and the rest of the team made up of weaklings. While this will allow some occasional success it is not enough to build the broad and diverse export base that MENA needs.

Notes

1. On intra-MENA trade, see inter alia Bolbol and Fatheldin (2005).
2. Cieslik and Hagemejer (2009) find that MENA-EU deals increased MENA imports from Europe but not MENA exports to the continent. Freund and Portugal (2013) find little export response to MENA's EU agreements, US agreements, and intraregional agreements. Nugent (2002) asks why MENA trades so little by investigating a number of trade agreements within the region. In most cases, the agreements did not appear to increase trade over the 1970–97 period.
3. Evidence of a similar pattern has been provided for an individual country like Peru (Volpe and Carballo 2008).
4. These stylized facts are robust to controlling for income levels and cross-sectoral specialization patterns.
5. The term "pricing to market" goes back to Krugman (1986) and refers to a practice whereby firms react to bilateral exchange-rate shocks by adjusting their FOB export price, creating wedges between domestic and FOB export prices (and between those across different destinations) rather than by passing through shocks to consumer prices.
6. The very fine level of disaggregation of the data, covering twelve countries including seven MENA countries, at different stages of development, enables a precise identification. In the econometric analysis the control for firm-product-destination and product-year fixed effects in the econometric regressions allows us to filter out many confounding factors that have only been imperfectly accounted for in other studies.
7. Estimates reported in the literature on industrial and emerging countries typically lie between 0.05 and 0.2.
8. The results are robust to controlling for country and product effects and accounting for variation in country and sector scale.
9. Freund and Pierola (2014) calculate the Balassa index of revealed comparative advantage (RCA) in 15 industries and determine the share of country industries that would lose RCA in the absence of superstars. The Balassa index compares the share of an industry in a country's aggregate exports with its share in world trade; comparative-advantage industries are those with a Balassa index above one.

References

Amiti, M., O. Itskhoki, and J. Konings. 2014. "Importers, Exporters and Exchange Rate Disconnect." *American Economic Review* 104 (7): 1942–78.

Asprilla, A., N. Berman, O. Cadot, and M. Jaud. 2014. "Pricing-to-Market, Trade Policy, and Market Power." Mimeo.

Atkeson, A., and A. Burstein. 2008. "Trade Costs, Pricing-to-Market, and International Relative Prices." *American Economic Review* 98: 1998–2031.

Auer, R., and R. Schoenle. 2013. "Market Structure and Exchange-Rate Pass-Through." Swiss National Bank and Brandeis University.

Behar, A., and C. Freund. 2011. "The Trade Performance of the Middle East and North Africa." Middle East and North Africa Working Paper 53, World Bank, Washington, DC.

Berman, N., P. Martin, and T. Mayer. 2012. "How Do Different Firms React to Exchange-Rate Changes?" *Quarterly Journal of Economics* 127: 437–92.

Bernard, A., B. Jensen, S. Redding, and P. Schott. 2007. "Firms in International Trade." *Journal of Economic Perspectives* 21 (3): 105–30.

Bertrand, M., F. Kramarz, A. Schoar, and D. Thesmar. 2007. "Politicians, Firms, and the Political Business Cycle: Evidence from France." PSE/University of Chicago.

Bolbol, Ali A., and A. Fatheldin. 2005. *Intra-Arab Exports and Direct Investments: An Empirical Analysis*. Arab Monetary Fund, Abu Dhabi.

Brunel, Claire, A. Fernandes, and M. Jaud. 2015. "Export Diversification in MENA: A Firm-Level Perspective." Mimeo.

Cebeci, T., A. Fernandes, C. Freund, and M. D. Pierola. 2012. "Exporter Dynamics Database." Working Paper Series 6229, World Bank, Washington DC.

Cieslik, A., and J. Hagemejer. 2009. "Assessing the Impact of the EU-Sponsored Trade Liberalization in the MENA Countries." *Journal of Economic Integration* 24: 343–68.

Diop, N., D. Marotta, and J. De Melo. 2012. *Natural Resource Abundance, Growth, and Diversification in the Middle East and North Africa: The Effects of Natural Resources and the Role of Policies*. Washington, DC : World Bank.

Feenstra, R., J. Gagnon, and M. Knetter. 1996. "Market Share and Exchange-Rate Pass-Through in World Automobile Trade." *Journal of International Economics* 40: 187–207.

Fernandes, Ana. 2014. "Exporters in MENA: Characterization and Benchmarking." Mimeo.

Freund, C., and M. Pierola. 2012. "Export Surges." *Journal of Development Economics* 97: 387–95.

———. 2014. "MENA's Export Subpar Stars." Mimeo.

———. Forthcoming. "Export Superstars." *The Review of Economics and Statistics*.

Freund, C., and A. Portugal. 2013. "Assessing MENA's Trade Agreements." In M. Gasiorek, ed., *The Arab Spring: Implications for Economic Integration*, a Voxeu book, Femise and CEPR.

Haidar, Jamal I. 2014. "Sanctions and Exports Deflection." Mimeo.

Krugman, Paul. 1986. "Pricing to Market When the Exchange Rate Changes." NBER Working Paper 1926, National Bureau of Economic Research, Boston, MA.

Mayer, T., and G. Ottaviano. 2007. *The Happy Few: The Internationalization of European Firms—New Facts Based on Firm-Level Evidence*. Paris: Sciences Po.

Nabli, M., J. Keller, C. Nassif, and C. Silva-Jauregui. 2006. "The Political Economy of Industrial Policy in the Middle East and North Africa." World Bank.

Nugent, Jeffrey B. 2002. "Why Does MENA Trade So Little?" University of Southern California, Los Angeles, CA.

Rouis, M., and S. Tabor. 2013. *Regional Economic Integration in the Middle East and North Africa: Beyond Trade Reforms*. Washington, DC: World Bank.

Volpe, Martinicus C., and J. Carballo. 2008. "Survival of New Exporters in Developing Countries: Does It Matter How They Diversify?" Working Paper Series IDB-WP-140, Inter-American Development Bank.

CHAPTER 3

Priced out of Global Markets

Key Messages

Why has the region failed to nurture a group of "world class" exporters in comparative-advantage sectors capable of lifting its export performance? Part of the problem is the lack of a competitive real exchange rate (RER). In this chapter we show how the deleterious effects of an uncompetitive currency can be traced all the way down to the level of the firm, hurting expansion at the intensive and extensive margin and preventing the emergence of export take-offs. In an increasingly competitive global environment, it is high time for Middle East and North Africa (MENA) governments to put export competitiveness at the heart of exchange-rate management.

Exchange Rate Policy in MENA

The single most important price that affects exporters large and small alike is the RER. As the RER appreciates, the price of domestic goods abroad increases and as a result the demand for them falls. The reverse happens in the domestic market. Foreign goods become relatively cheaper and demand for them rises encouraging spending on imports.

Pegged nominal exchange rates can be especially prone to the risk of overvaluation. In MENA, while a number of countries have made some progress in adopting market-based monetary policy instruments, exchange rate regimes in the region are still predominantly pegged regimes, either against the US dollar (Bahrain, Kuwait, Oman, Qatar, Saudi Arabia, the United Arab Emirates, Iraq, and Lebanon), or against a combination of the U.S. dollar and the euro (Libya, Kuwait, Morocco). Pegging the nominal exchange rates causes the RER to appreciate, each time inflation at home is higher than in the country issuing the anchor currency. When currencies become overvalued, realignment requires downward adjustment in wages and prices, but prices tend to be sticky downward. Thus, overvaluation owing to fixed exchange rates can plague economies for many years, and in some cases leads to economically costly currency crises.

In a world where a number of Asian countries' currencies are estimated to be significantly undervalued against the dollar—moderately to severely in the case of Singapore and Taiwan, China and mildly relative to those of Japan, China, and Hong Kong SAR, China (Cline 2014)—MENA exporters competing against Asia are at a direct disadvantage. Reforming the exchange rate policy to allow flexibility is important in MENA to ensure the most important price in an economy is set appropriately.

Under-Exporting and Over-Importing

The gravity equation, workhorse of empirical trade analysis, is widely used to benchmark trade openness and assess the extent of barriers to trade, taking into account gravity-driven regularities in the geographical patterns of international trade flows. Here, we use it to highlight a particular feature of MENA's trade performance—the imbalance between its relative trade performance on the export and import sides, controlling for the proximity of the European Union (EU), a very large market. We show that the gravity-based evidence points in the direction of an underlying macroeconomic imbalance rather than high trade costs across the board.

Without controlling for any covariates, MENA's non-natural-resources trade-to-GDP ratio is only three percentage points less than the worldwide average of 35 percent (Behar and Freund 2011). However, the proper benchmark should not be average trade but the average trade predicted by a gravity equation, controlling for partners' size, income, and "remoteness." Table 3.1 measures the extent of MENA's under-trading by reporting the coefficients on regional fixed effects in cross-sectional gravity equations for different country groupings: three MENA groupings and two other groupings of countries in the EU's periphery.[1] The coefficients reported in table 3.1 can be interpreted as the deviation in percentage terms of predicted trade from the benchmark.[2] As a whole, MENA under-exports significantly and by a wide margin, –55 percent for overall trade (see column 1 in panel a). Considering non-commodity trade, MENA's exports to the outside world are only one-third of their potential in recent years. For the MENA-4 group, composed of the Arab Republic of Egypt, Jordan, Morocco, and Tunisia, the effect is smaller (see column 2 in panel c), but this may be due to a lower number of observations. Considering imports, the results suggest that MENA does not under-import and the MENA-4, in particular, over-import significantly and by a wide margin, 37 percent for non-commodity trade.

As to regional trade, the MENA-4 actually *over-trade* among themselves—a finding that stands in stark contrast to the standard narrative of trade in the region. While the positive estimate for intra-MENA-4 trade is surprising, it should be interpreted with the logic of the gravity equation in mind. Given MENA's proximity to the EU a very large trading bloc, the gravity model predicts that it should trade mostly with the EU and little with itself. Indeed, MENA's "multilateral resistance term" is found to be small relative to that of other regions (see Behar and Freund 2011).[3] Thus, the trade of the MENA-4 with themselves is higher than predicted given that it is predicted to be small, but it is not high relative to an absolute benchmark.

Table 3.1 Is MENA Under-Trading? Results from a Gravity Equation

	(1)	(2)	(3)	(4)	(5)
Country groupings	MENA-All	MENA-4	MENA-Others	EU Periphery1	EU Periphery2
Sample period	2005–09	2005–09	2005–09	2001–03	2003–06
Panel a: Overall trade					
Exports	−0.55***	−0.14	−0.59***	0.13*	0.19*
Imports	−0.04	0.36***	−0.12	−0.31***	−0.28***
Regional trade	0.045***	2.23***	0.33***	0.57***	1.26*
Panel b: Non-petroleum trade					
Exports	−0.64**	−0.35***	−0.63***	0.039	−0.37***
Imports	0.22**	0.37**	0.14	−0.11	−0.33***
Regional trade	−0.24***	1.06***	−0.54***	0.37	0.25***
Panel c: Non-commodity trade					
Exports	−0.69***	−0.03	−0.77***	0.02	0.002
Imports	0.09	0.41**	0.021	−0.11	−0.29***
Regional trade	−0.007***	2.92***	−0.49***	0.49	0.78*

Source: Estimation based on the CEPII's BACI database.
Note: Panel (a) reports results on all trade; panel (b) excludes oil products (HS chapters 25–27); and panel (c) excludes all commodity trade. The effects reported are in percentage terms. The different country groupings are: "MENA-all" includes all MENA countries; "MENA-4" is composed of the Arab Republic of Egypt, Jordan, Morocco, and Tunisia; "MENA-other" is composed of the rest of the region; Eastern Periphery 1 (EP1) includes the countries that joined the EU in 2004: Cyprus, Czech Republic, Estonia, Hungary, Latvia, Lithuania, Malta, Poland, Slovak Republic, Slovenia; and Eastern Periphery 2 (EP2), includes countries that joined the EU in 2007: Bulgaria, Romania, Croatia, plus the former Yugoslav Republic of Macedonia and Turkey. Significance at the 10, 5, and 1 percent levels are denoted by *, **, and ***, respectively.

Another result that emerges from table 3.1 is the opposite signs on export and import performance, which differs from what we observe for the other two EU peripheries groups. If trade costs were unusually high for MENA countries, we would expect on average both imports and exports to be affected. Yet this is not the case. In fact, figure 3.1 shows that the MENA-4 countries perform better than predicted at their income level for four important trade-cost indicators: the logistics performance index, the delay and cost to export, and the number of documents required to export.

The simultaneous occurrence of under-exporting and over-importing, especially in contrast with the other EU peripheries, is more suggestive of macroeconomic distortions, such as real-exchange rate overvaluation, than of excessive trade costs across the board. This interpretation is consistent with the finding that between 1980 and 2010, the RERs were frequently overvalued in a large number of countries in MENA, and that this overvaluation had adverse effects on the region's competitiveness in the manufacturing sector (Diop, Marotta, and De Melo 2012). Taking the case of Morocco, over the period 1970–2005, the Moroccan Dirham has been overvalued on average by 24 percent, with potentially large consequences for the region's export performance (see de Melo and Ugarte 2011, with an approach similar to that of Rodrik 2008).[4]

Figure 3.1 Trade Costs in MENA

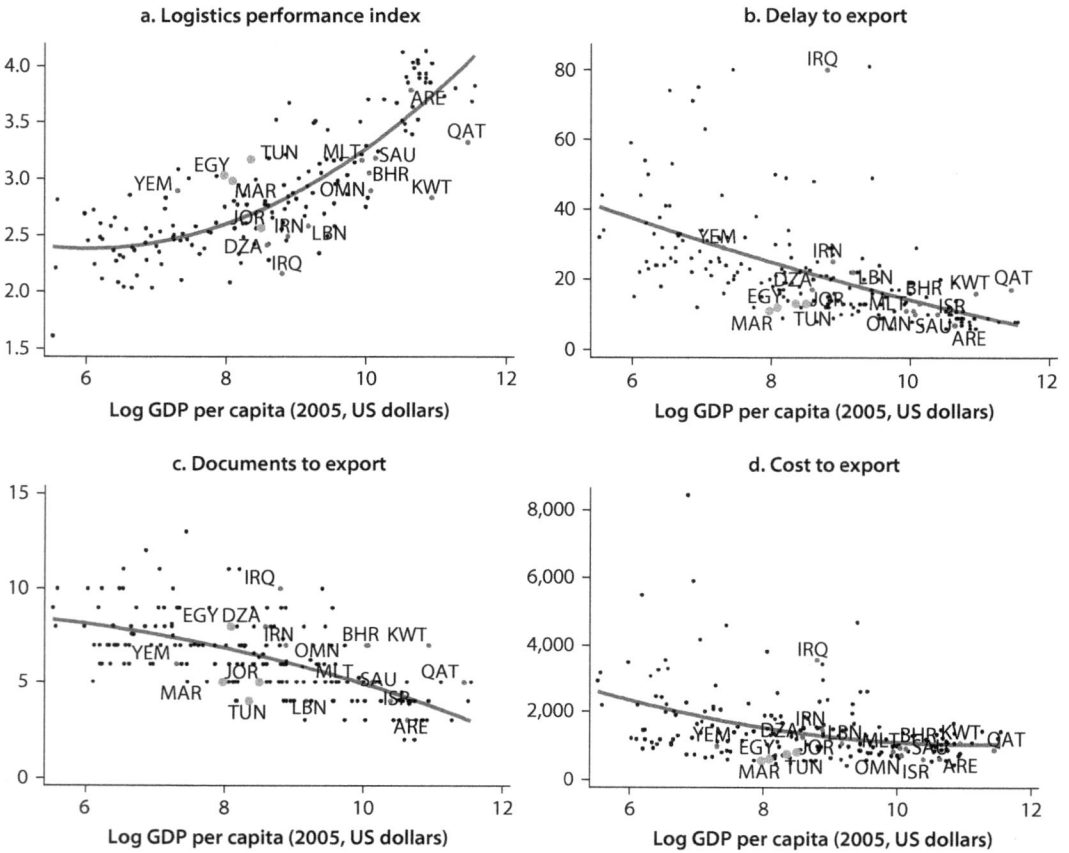

a. Logistics performance index

b. Delay to export

c. Documents to export

d. Cost to export

Source: Wood and Yang 2014.
Note: The MENA-4 group including the Arab Republic of Egypt, Jordan, Morocco, and Tunisia are in orange, other MENA countries in blue.

Overvaluation Hurts

At the aggregate level, there is evidence that "growth accelerations" correlate with periods of substantial and sustained currency undervaluation (Hausmann, Pritchett, and Rodrik 2005; see also Rajan and Subramanian 2007; Rodrik 2008). A similar argument has been made about "export surges," seven-year growth accelerations of aggregate manufactured exports. The RER is the most important variable in predicting export booms (Freund and Pierola 2012). In industrial countries, the exchange rate tends to depreciate by about 15 percent on average prior to an export boom. The role of the exchange rate is even more pronounced in developing countries, where a 20 percent real depreciation precedes an export surge on average. The MENA countries fit this pattern.

In a cross-country sample from 1980 to 2006, MENA countries had 16 export booms according to their filter. Table 3.2 reports the breakdown by country as well as the date the surge started, the variation in the RER during the previous

Table 3.2 Exchange Rate and Export Surges in MENA

Country	Number of export surge (1)	Year of surge (2)	Percentage change in RER over five years before surge (3)	Percentage change in exports over five years after surge (4)	Percentage change in number of trials over five years after surge (5)
Bahrain	1	1988	17	26	19
Egypt, Arab Rep.	2	1987, 2000	−27	96	50
Israel	2	1986, 2004	2	54	2
Jordan	2	1984, 1998	6	75	38
Kuwait	1	1998	−5	97	16
Lebanon	1	2000	−16	65	48
Morocco	1	1986	44	120	41
Oman	1	1992	4	42	33
Qatar	1	1997	−10	67	29
Saudi Arabia	1	1986	116	64	−7
Syrian Arab Rep.	1	1990	10	71	90
Tunisia	1	1986	22	90	35
United Arab Emirates	1	1988	12	94	47
MENA	16	1984–2006	13	74	32
Developing (excluding MENA)	59	1984–2006	34	158	41
Industrialized (excluding MENA)	16	1984–2006	9	80	8

Source: Calculations based on Freund and Pierola 2012.
Note: The data used spans the period 1980–2006. An increase in the real exchange rate is a depreciation of the home currency. Trials are defined as the log of the average number of new product-market trials in each year in each country. We then take the average across MENA countries, non-MENA developing countries, and non-MENA industrialized countries.

five years, and the change in export values in the five years following the surge. Table 3.2 suggests that on average the currencies in MENA countries depreciated by nearly 13 percent in real terms in the five years preceding the surge (see column 3). This is less than in other developing countries, where the home currency depreciated on average by almost 35 percent. The depreciation in RER is associated with an increase in manufacturing exports in all countries, although the increase is far more pronounced in developing countries than in MENA and industrialized countries. In MENA, exports increased by 74 percent over the five years following the initiation of the surge, about the same as industrialized countries and far less than the 158 percent found in other developing countries (see column 4). Table 3.2 also reports the evolution of the extensive margin of exports in the five years following the initiation of the export surge in MENA countries, other developing, and developed countries. Depreciation stimulates entry into new export products and new markets. However, in MENA, the number of new product-market trials increased by 32 percent over the five years following the initiation of the surge—10 percent less than the average increase found for non-MENA developing.

Among MENA countries Morocco is particularly interesting. The Dirham remained overvalued in all years over the period 1970–2005, aside from a brief

Champions Wanted • http://dx.doi.org/10.1596/978-1-4648-0460-1

period in the mid-1980s. Not surprisingly, that was also the period of most rapid manufacturing trade growth in Morocco. The Morocco export surge started in 1986 (see table 3.2).

More recent evidence on Morocco using product-level data confirms the effect of real overvaluation on export performance albeit with some nuances. While at the aggregate level, a weakly negative relationship exists between exchange-rate changes and exports; results are stronger at the industry level (Crozet and Taglioni 2014). For example, a 10 percent real depreciation would raise Moroccan exports by 4 percent on average across products defined at the 6-digit level of the Harmonized System (HS) classification. The supply response is stronger in the textile and apparel and footwear sectors, where a 10 percent RER depreciation would raise exports by 6.9 percent and 10.1 percent, respectively. In terms of its impact on export prices, a 10 percent depreciation would raise Moroccan product export prices by only 1.3 percent, suggesting that 87 percent of the shocks are passed through to consumers. A consequence of this strong pass-through is that the impact on quantities exported and hence potentially employment is large.

However, it is at the firm level that export decisions are made. How strong is the evidence for this type of effect at the firm level? Evidence on Morocco suggests that the changes in the bilateral RER essentially affect aggregate exports through the intensive margin. A 10 percent decrease in Morocco's bilateral exchange rate increases firm-level exports by 2.7 percent on average—a relatively small impact compared to the aggregate estimates of 4 percent on average across products, or 6.9 and 10.1 percent in the textile and apparel, and footwear sectors, respectively. Most of the firm-level adjustment to RER changes is on quantities (62 percent), with only 38 percent of the overall impact on prices.

Most interesting is the impact of RER changes on the extensive margin. In Morocco, a 10 percent RER depreciation raises the probability of exporting at the firm-product-destination level by 0.2 percentage points only and cuts the probability of exit by 0.6 percentage points, a much lower elasticity than that experienced by French firms (Berman, Martin, and Mayer 2012).[5] This lack of response at the extensive margin contrasts with the finding in Freund and Pierola (2012) that the discovery of new products and new markets is an important component of export surges in developing countries—accounting for over 40 percent of total manufacturing export growth during the surge. However, they should be interpreted keeping in mind that both sets of results are obtained using different time periods. While Morocco experienced a large currency depreciation in the mid-1980s, triggering a large and sudden export growth acceleration, the bilateral RER has only experienced small variations over the period 2000–12. Rather than suggesting RER does not affect the extensive margin, they suggest that there may be threshold effects: whereby only large enough RER depreciations have large impacts on exports. At the firm-level, Chatterjee, Dix-Carneiro, and Vichyanond (2013) provide empirical evidence in the case of Brazil, that following real currency depreciations firms expand not only their volume of exports but their product scope too. The intuition is that when the home currency is strong, export profitability is weak and the firm concentrates on its most profitable core product. As the home currency depreciates, the export profitability rises and the firm moves down the product ladder, adding more and more marginally profitable products.[6]

Taken together, these results highlight the importance of a competitive currency for both firms and aggregate export performance. In this respect, many governments in MENA that have allowed their bilateral exchange rates to get overvalued over the past decades, have indeed done a huge disservice to their exporters.

Notes

1. All specifications are based on ordinary least squares (OLS) estimation on nonzero trade flows and therefore pick only volume differences between existing partners (the intensive margin) but differ by including different dummies marking oil exporters.

2. The deviation of predicted trade from the benchmark is equal to $e^{\beta}-1$ where β is a fixed-effect coefficient on the relevant regional grouping, either on the exporting side (β_{exp}), importing side (β_{imp}), or both (β_{Pair}). The deviation of intra-regional trade from the benchmark is computed as $e^{(\beta_{exp}+\beta_{imp}+\beta_{pair})}-1$.

3. Trade between two countries depends not only on the absolute cost of trading, which is known as bilateral resistance and is proxied by distance and other variables in gravity models, but on the cost of trading relative to the costs of trading with other countries, which is known as multilateral resistance. Failure to account for these so-called "third country" effects can lead to biased estimates and comparative statistics (Behar and Nelson 2009).

4. IMF (2014) notes that Tunisia's and Morocco's real effective exchange rates (REERs) have slightly depreciated since 2005, but it also shows evidence of rising current-account deficits (from 2 percent of GDP in 2007 to 8 percent for Tunisia and from 0 to 8 percent for Morocco) as well as declining reserves (from seven to four months' worth of imports for Morocco over the same period).

5. Regressions excluding Eurozone destinations, as the Dirham is indexed on a basket of currencies with an 80 percent weight on the euro, report larger but still small effects. This suggests that part of the reason behind the small effect may be the lack of variation over time in Morocco bilateral RER.

6. In a Melitz model, only firm-level productivity is stochastic, so the expansion/contraction of product scope in Chatterjee, Dix-Carneiro, and Vichyanond (2013) has no "self-discovery" dimension; but one could extend the framework along Hausmann-Rodrik lines where firms discover their own capabilities, product by product, until one of them hits a home run. As the currency depreciates, the probability of such a success rises with the number of trials, which itself rises with the number of firms times the number of additional products by firm, a very large number.

References

Behar, A., and C. Freund. 2011. "The Trade Performance of the Middle East and North Africa." Middle East and North Africa Working Paper 53, World Bank, Washington, DC.

Behar, A., and B. D. Nelson. 2009. "Trade Flows, Multilateral Resistance, and Firm Heterogeneity." *The Review of Economics and Statistics* 96 (3): 538–49.

Berman, N., P. Martin, and T. Mayer. 2012. "How Do Different Firms React to Exchange-Rate Changes?" *Quarterly Journal of Economics* 127: 437–92.

Chatterjee, A., R. Dix-Carneiro, and J. Vichyanond. 2013. "Multi-Product Firms and Exchange-Rate Fluctuations." *American Economic Journal* 5 (2): 77–110.

Cline, William R. 2014. "Estimates of Fundamental Equilibrium Exchange Rates, May 2014." Policy brief PB14-16, Peterson Institute for International Economics, Washington, DC.

Crozet, M., and D. Taglioni. 2014. "The Reaction of Moroccan Exporters to Real Exchange Rates Changes." Mimeo.

De Melo, J., and C. Ugarte. 2011. "Resource Abundance and Growth: Benchmarking MENA with the Rest of the World." In *Natural Resource Abundance, Growth, and Diversification in the Middle East and North Africa: The Effects of Natural Resources and the Role of Policies*, edited by N. Diop, D. Marotta, and J. de Melo. Washington, DC: World Bank.

Diop, N., D. Marotta, and J. De Melo. 2012. *Natural Resource Abundance, Growth, and Diversification in the Middle East and North Africa: The Effects of Natural Resources and the Role of Policies*. Washington, DC: World Bank.

Freund, C., and M. Pierola. 2012. "Export Surges." *Journal of Development Economics* 97: 387–95.

Freund, C., and M. D. Pierola. 2014. "MENA's Export Subpar Stars." Mimeo.

Hausmann, R., L. Pritchett, and D. Rodrik. 2005. "Growth Accelerations." *Journal of Economic Growth* 10: 303–29.

IMF (International Monetary Fund). 2014. *Toward New Horizons: Arab Economic Transformation Amid Political Transitions*. Washington, DC: IMF.

Melitz, Marc J. 2003. "The Impact of Trade on Intra-Industry Reallocations and Aggregate Industry Productivity." *Econometrica* 71: 1695–725.

Rajan, R., and A. Subramanian. 2007. "Aid, Dutch Disease and Manufacturing Growth." International Monetary Fund, Washington, DC.

Rodrik, Dani. 2008. "The Real Exchange Rate and Economic Growth." *Brookings Papers on Economic Activity* 39: 365–439.

Wood C., and J. Yang. 2014. "Export Performance and Specialization—The Role of Financial Sector Development and Governance in MENA." Mimeo.

CHAPTER 4

Getting Policy Right

Key Messages

The lack of heavy weight exporters at the top of the distribution also reflects the region's failure to push for trade and business climate reforms energetically. In this chapter we show that in an already competition-deficient environment, higher-than-average tariffs and restrictive non-tariff measures (NTMs) have further reduced domestic competition and thus export competitiveness. The high tariffs on intermediate products have also hampered firms' productivity and export growth. In addition, contrary to widely-held views, regulatory modernization can help domestic firms overcome managerial failures and upgrade quality, in turn raising their performance.

The Policy Environment in MENA

Middle East and North Africa (MENA) is a region where an effective competition policy has failed to emerge (World Bank 2009, 2014). This is partly due to the presence of state-owned enterprises, as well as the prevalence of political connections, particularly in non-tradable sectors. This lack of competition has important implications for performance. At the sector level in Tunisia, reductions in price-cost margins, implying increased levels of competition intensity, correlated with large increases in the subsequent level and growth of labor productivity (World Bank 2013). At the firm-level in MENA countries, the uneven, unpredictable, and discriminatory implementation of policies has had deleterious consequences for private sector dynamism, specifically the entry of new firms, productivity growth, and job creation (World Bank 2014).

In this context, pushing for trade and business climate reforms is key as they have deep impacts on domestic competition allowing the most efficient firms to replace the least efficient ones within sectors, in turn raising productivity, competitiveness, and job creation. Yet, the consensus in the literature is that the MENA region has failed to pursue trade reforms energetically (Bensassi et al. 2012; Rouis and Tabor 2013).

Figure 4.1 shows that tariffs in MENA have been falling less rapidly than in other regions, even for Morocco and Tunisia, the region's best performers.

Figure 4.1 Comparative Evolution of Average Tariffs, 1980s, 1990s, 2000s

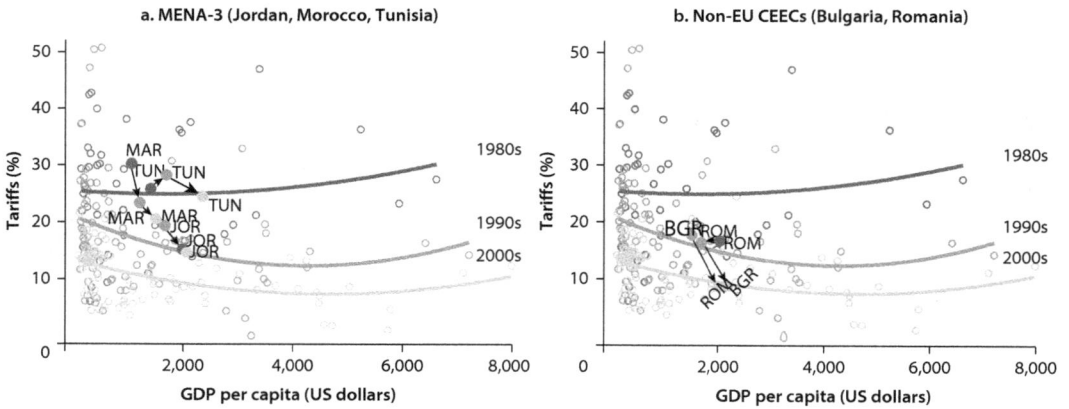

a. MENA-3 (Jordan, Morocco, Tunisia)   b. Non-EU CEECs (Bulgaria, Romania)

GDP per capita (US dollars)   GDP per capita (US dollars)

Source: Computation using tariffs data from the TRAINS database.
Note: Curves are quadratic polynomial fits for worldwide average tariffs in the 1980s, 1990s, and 2000s, respectively. Sample truncated at $10,000 at PPP for better readability. The Arab Republic of Egypt's tariff data is too fragmentary to be comparable to other countries and is thus not included.

Figure 4.2 NTMs in MENA: From Command-and-Control to Regulations

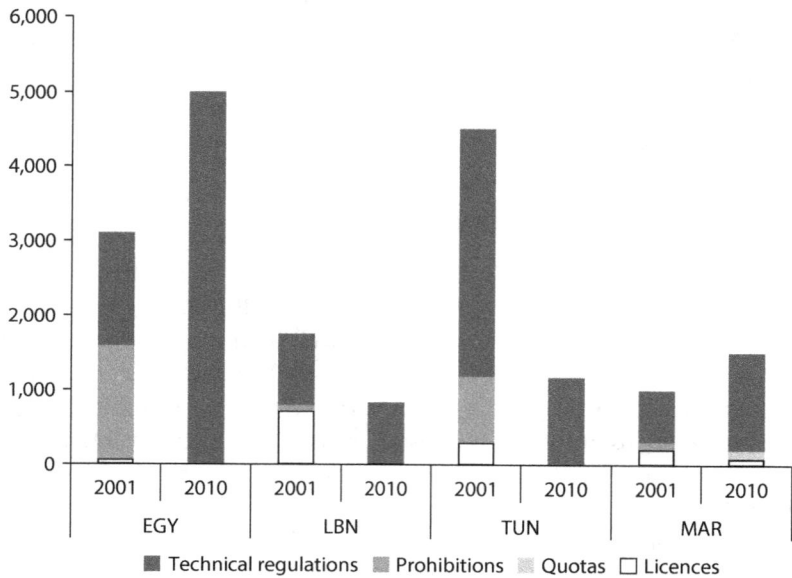

■ Technical regulations ▒ Prohibitions ░ Quotas □ Licences

Sources: Data for 2001 are from TRAINS; data for 2010 are from World Bank-UNCTAD multilateral NTM database.
Note: The height of the bars is the frequency ratio of NTMs (proportion of HS6 products covered by one or more NTM).

By comparison, countries like Romania or Bulgaria liberalized much more energetically before their accession to the EU (panel b). In other words, MENA's best compare poorly with the Central and East European Coalition's (CEEC) most tardy reformers.

NTMs have also been a complex agenda. Figure 4.2 compares the incidence and the type of NTMs imposed by MENA countries between 2001 and 2010.

It is suggestive of a modernization of the regulatory apparatus with traditional command-and-control instruments like quotas and prohibitions, prominent trade policy tools in 2001, being largely replaced by regulatory measures by 2010. However, it also shows in the case of the Arab Republic of Egypt and Morocco, an increase in the share of products actually concerned with NTMs.

Tariffs, NTMs, and Market Power

How much of a problem is MENA's failure to reduce tariffs and restrictive NTMs as rapidly as the rest of the world? Here again, the firm-level evidence can help us understand how trade policy affects competition and market structure and how the effects of different trade-policy instruments play out.

Using our previous approach that consists of assessing the impact of trade policy on market structure through firm-level pricing behavior, we find that, on our entire sample of countries, including seven MENA countries, trade policy indeed affects market structure. Higher tariffs reduce the market share of outside exporters through "rent-shifting" effects (Brander and Spencer 1984) thereby limiting their ability to price to market. By contrast, if NTMs are enforced in a non-discriminatory manner in the destination market—as required by the World Trade Organization's (WTO) "national treatment" clauses whereby imported and domestically-produced products must be treated alike—they do not shift rents, but rather force out the least efficient firms who cannot cope with the costs imposed by the new regulations, raising the market power of the remaining firms (domestic and foreign alike), in turn raising their incentive to engage in pricing-to-market (PTM).[1] In short, we would expect exporters to engage in less PTM in markets where tariffs are high and in more PTM in destination markets where NTMs are applied in a non-discriminatory way. The extent of exporters' pricing-to-market on MENA markets can thus be read as an indication of whether these markets have high tariff protection and apply safety and technical regulations in a discriminatory way or not.

Over the whole sample, we find that these effects are large in magnitude and highly significant (see figure 4.3). For instance, faced with a 10 percent deprecia-tion of its home currency, an exporter selling a product tariff-free in a given desti-nation would raise his home-currency price by 1.7 percent, i.e., an elasticity to exchange of 17 percent. Faced with the same depreciation on a destination where he sold the same product with a 10 percent tariff he would raise it by only 1 per-cent. When the tariff reaches 20–25 percent there is no significant PTM left any-more. As for NTMs, PTM is significantly stronger in markets with high levels of NTMs. The effects are also quantitatively significant albeit slightly smaller than in the case of tariffs. Moving from zero to a 10 percent ad valorem equivalent raises the price elasticity to exchange rate from 9 to 14 percent. On MENA markets, we find suggestive evidence that foreign exporters engage if anything in less PTM.

These results imply that MENA's lingering tariff protection and restrictive technical or sanitary regulations, significantly discriminates against foreign pro-ducers as approximated by their ability to price to market. As tariffs never make

Champions Wanted • http://dx.doi.org/10.1596/978-1-4648-0460-1

Figure 4.3 Trade Policy and Pricing-to-Market

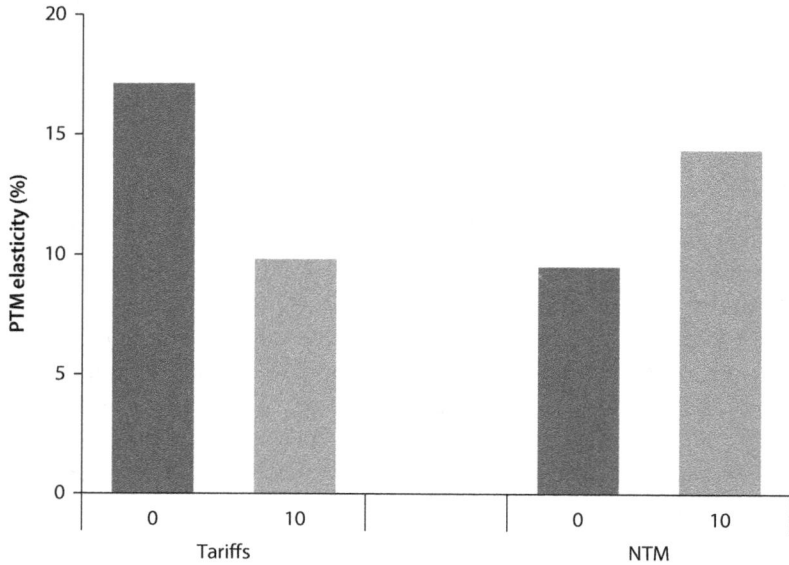

Source: Asprilla et al. 2014.
Note: The figure shows the results of regressions on the full sample of countries of the log of export unit
values on the log of the real bilateral exchange rate and its interaction with the log of bilateral tariffs, or
alternatively with a measure of ad-valorem equivalent of NTM, controlling for firm-product-destination and
origin-year fixed effects. The height of the bar reports the rate of PTM in percent, i.e., the exporter price
elasticity to exchange rate, under two scenarios: 0 and 10 percent for each type of instrument. The sample
covers 12 low- and middle-income countries, including Bangladesh (2006–11), Chile (2004–09), Jordan
(2004–11), Kenya (2006–11), Kuwait (2009–10), Lebanon (2009–10), Mexico (2001–09), Morocco (2003–11),
Rwanda (2006–11), Tanzania (2006–11), Uganda (2005–11), and the Republic of Yemen (2007–11), with data
at the firm-HS 8-destination-year level for different time periods for each country.

markets more competitive, the market power taken away from foreign producers
must be captured by domestic ones.

Tariffs Limit Global Value Chains

The inefficiencies generated by high tariffs are compounded when they affect
intermediate products. As stages of production are spread across national boundaries, changes in trade costs can have a magnified impact on trade flows, because
they are incurred each time the good is traded back and forth between countries.
The presence of importing and exporting activities within firms is evidence of
this fragmentation of production. In Tunisia 42 percent of exporters also import
and 82 percent of importers also export. As a comparator, in the US 41 percent
of exporters are importers and 79 percent of importers export. In contrast, in
Morocco for which we also have the matched import-export data at the firm
level, the distribution is reversed with a higher share of exporters that also
import, 65 percent, and a lower share of importers that export, only 22 percent.
This difference partly reflects the existence of special economic zones, where

Figure 4.4 Trade Protection on Final and Intermediate Inputs in MENA

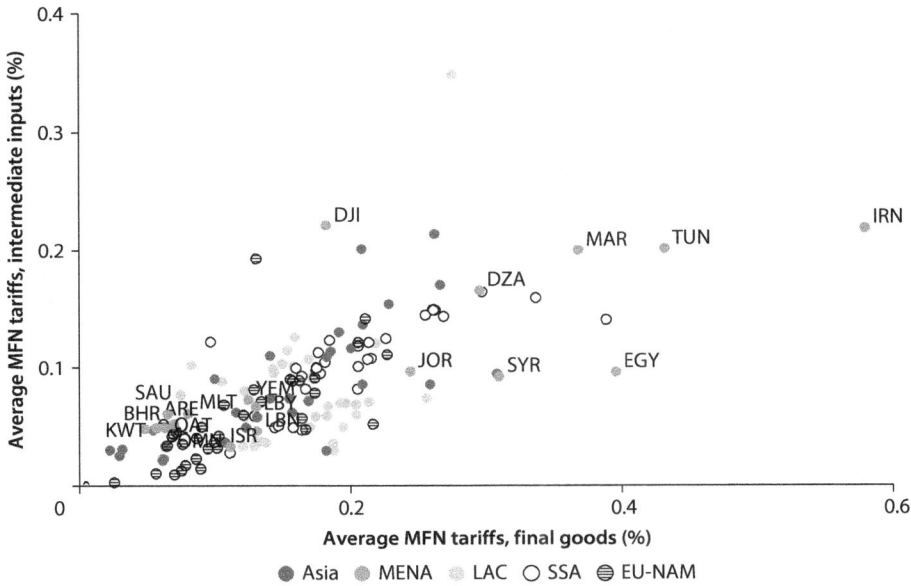

Source: Calculations using data on Most Favored Nation (MFN) tariffs from TRAINS over the period 1995 to 2012.
Note: For each country-pair-product and year we compute the bilateral applied tariff and then take the average by country and type of goods over the period in order to smooth out missing values.

domestic firms mainly do light transformation and mostly assembly of high-value intermediate inputs made elsewhere.

Figure 4.4 provides evidence that MENA countries, especially those with a strong manufacturing base, are applying higher-than-average tariffs on their intermediate inputs. The figure plots the average most favored nation (MFN) tariffs for final goods against the average MFN tariffs for intermediate inputs by country over the period 1995–2012.[2] The lowest levels of MFN tariffs are observed in developed countries (e.g., 3.1 percent in Japan), while North African resource-poor countries including the MENA-4, Egypt, Morocco, Tunisia, and Jordan and South Asian countries have the highest (over 20 percent in India, Tunisia, or Morocco). By contrast resource-rich MENA countries plus Lebanon and Israel are among the most open economies.

Given imported inputs are becoming increasingly important in global trade, how much of a problem is MENA-4's failure to reduce tariffs on intermediate goods as rapidly as the rest of the world? A large and growing body of academic literature shows that access to imported inputs does more to expand firm productivity than exporting (Amiti and Konings 2007; Kasahara and Rodrigue 2008; Bas and Strauss-Kahn 2011) and helps firms expand their export volume, improve the quality of their products (Bas 2012; Feng, Li, and Swenson 2012; Manova and Zhang 2012; Bastos, Silva, and Verhoogen 2013; Chevassus-Lozza et al. 2013), and diversify their export bundle (Goldberg et al. 2010). In Morocco, between 2002 and 2010, a substantial reduction in intermediate input tariffs (both MFN and preferential following the implementation of several trade agree-ments) resulted in significant expansion of firms' export value and destination reached (Cruz and Bussolo 2014, estimate an elasticity of 0.9 and 0.8, respectively). In addition, exporters in sectors that experienced the highest tariff reductions improved their chances of survival past their first year. In addition, the relatively rapid growth of exports from firms in export processing zones, where compa-nies are able to import duty-free inputs for their exported goods, further supports this idea that an improved access to intermediate inputs helps firms' export performance.

Using detailed matched import-export data at the firm-product-partner country level between 2002 and 2010 for Morocco, we are able to examine in greater details how better access to intermediate inputs contribute to firms' subsequent export growth, diversification, and product quality. Figure 4.5 offers suggestive evidence of the quality premium associated with importing higher-quality inputs. The difference in export unit values between firms that both import and export and firms that only export is large and most importantly has been increasing over time.

One difficulty with this exercise is the potential for reverse causality and omitted-variable bias. Better-managed firms are likely to have both good sourcing and efficient export strategies. We work around this issue, by instrumenting the quality of imported intermediates by the revealed comparative advantage (RCA) of the country supplying the given intermediate products. The intuition

Figure 4.5 Imported Inputs and Export Prices in Morocco

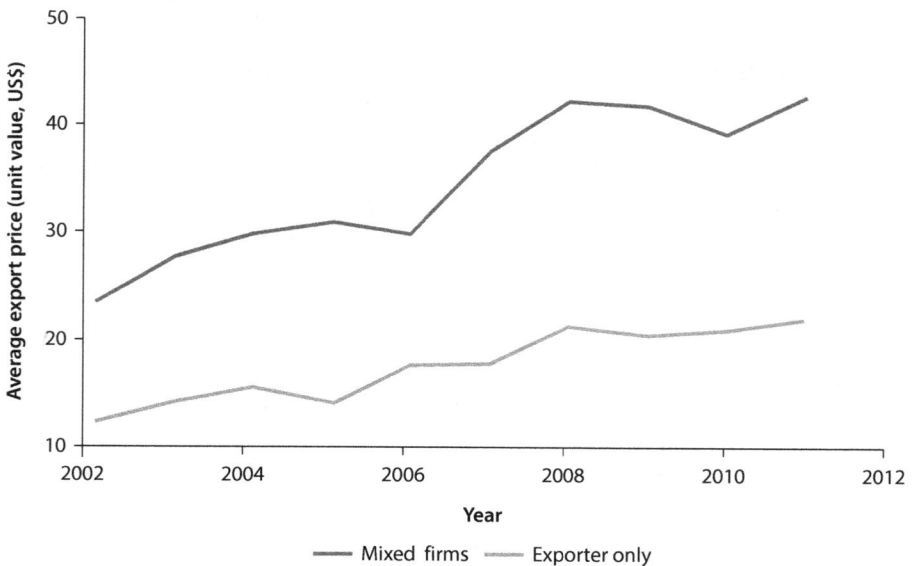

Source: Le Bris, Disdier, and Jaud 2014.
Note: Unit values are computed at the firm-HS 8-destination level and averaged by firm type and year. Mixed firms are firms that both import intermediate inputs and export.

is the following: If a Moroccan garment producer buys his fabric from Vietnam and the RCA of Vietnam in fabric increases over time, then the inference is that the Moroccan firm is getting better quality fabric.[3] The results suggest strong linkages from imported input to export at the extensive margin (product and destination diversification) as well as the intensive (export growth) and "quality" (unit values) margins.

These results suggest that access to better inputs through a reduction of import tariffs has important consequences for exports. Their implications also extend to locally sourced inputs. In fact, for firms that are not located in export processing zones nor engaged in global value chains (GVC) with assistance from their buyers (Kee and Tang 2012), identifying reliable intermediate providers willing to supply them can be a challenge, as the most reputable ones will prefer to service large and established clients. In addition, even if individual firms are able to source high-quality inputs from abroad, transport costs and the increasing prevalence of "just-in-time" production imply that a lack of high-quality locally available inputs is likely to hinder the ability of even the most talented firms to succeed. Relatedly, the upgrading of downstream firms or the entry of foreign companies is likely to generate pressure on local suppliers to improve quality (Javorcik 2004; Kugler 2006). In Bangladesh, the presence of foreign companies in the downstream manufacturing sector improved the efficiency, product quality, and variety of upstream suppliers. This in turn had positive spillovers on the productivity and export performance of domestic firms in the downstream sector, as they could source those better inputs locally (Kee 2015).

Regulatory Convergence as Export Promotion

Like tariff liberalization, progress made on streamlining NTMs has been limited. In some cases, convergence with EU regulations under Euromed agreements has been viewed as a commitment mechanism to move ahead on regulatory reform.

Figure 4.6 plots countries with available NTM data, according to their similarities and differences in their use of NTM regulations across products (see appendix C for details on the formula of the "regulatory distance"). Figure 4.6 can be thought of as a "regulatory distance map," with countries close to each other applying similar NTMs across products, whereas countries at the graph's periphery apply NTMs in idiosyncratic ways. The majority of countries form a "core" with closely related regulations. By contrast, despite regulatory harmonization with the EU, Morocco remains an outlier, with a large regulatory distance relative to the EU as well as from other trading partners.

In this section, we focus on two MENA countries, Egypt and Morocco, for which novel NTM data was collected and matched with firm-level trade data, and provide new evidence on the different channels through which regulations may affect firms' performance. We start by running a standard gravity model on a combined dataset of Egyptian firm customs data with data on specific trade concerns raised in the sanitary and phytosanitary (SPS) committees at the World Trade Organization (WTO). Results suggest that SPS measures reduce firms'

Figure 4.6 Cross-Country Regulatory Distances

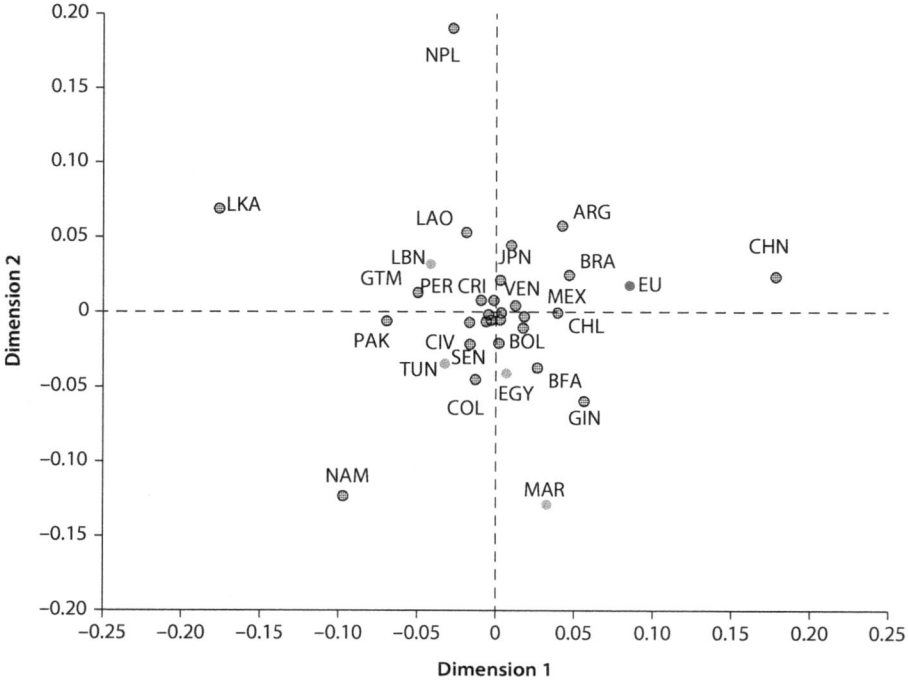

Source: Calculations based on UNCTAD multilateral NTM database for 2010.
Note: The Kruskal's stress, computed as the square root of a normalized residual sum of squares, is a measure of badness-of-fit, with larger values indicating worse fit. Kruskal's stress measures the distortion imposed by two-dimensional projection of a bilateral distance matrix. Here the Kruskal's stress value is 0.208.

export performance mostly at the extensive margin. When faced with an SPS regulation in a given product and market, an Egyptian exporter is less likely, by almost 5 percent, to enter that market. This negative effect varies with firm size, with smaller exporters being hit the hardest (El-Enbaby, Hendy, and Zaki 2014). The intuition for this result is that larger and more productive exporters are able to better absorb the additional costs imposed by regulations in their destination markets, possibly by mobilizing resources from non SPS-imposing sectors and destinations. This in turn allows them to enjoy lower competition in that market and make higher profits (Fontagné et al. 2013).

Morocco provides another interesting case study. Largely mandated under the Association Agreement with the EU, Morocco has embarked on a process of regulatory convergence towards EU. regulations. Figure 4.7 reports the evolution between 1990 and 2012 of the count of harmonization of domestic NTMs with the EU regulations. Strikingly domestic NTM harmonization has occurred in waves, with the largest number in 1993 (70 measures harmonized), 1996 (125), 2000 (173), 2003 (173), 2006 (147), and 2012 (91).

As convergence towards EU regulations is expected of other EU partners, Morocco provides a convenient laboratory to test its effects. Moreover, as

Figure 4.7 Harmonization of Moroccan NTMs with EU Regulations

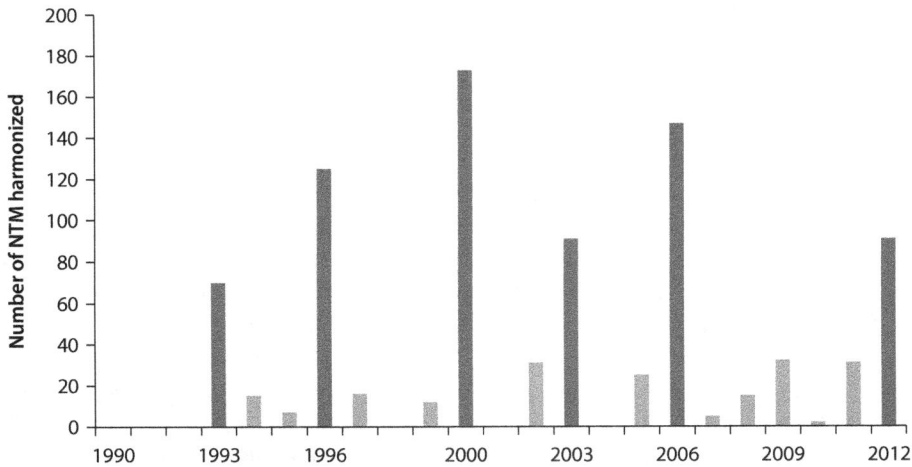

Sources: Augier, Cadot, and Dovis 2014; Dovis and Jaud 2014.

Morocco's regulations prior to harmonization were largely outdated and unevenly enforced, there is a reasonable presumption that new (harmonized) regulations are stricter, *de jure* or *de facto*, than the old ones they replaced. By combining this information with firm-level census and trade data we are able to examine the impact of standard harmonization not only on firms' export performance, but also on firms' non-trade performance, including profits and productivity. Box 4.1 summarizes the different channels through which standard harmonization may affect firms' performance.

We first uncover an "export promotion" effect of regulatory harmonization (Dovis and Jaud 2014). We find that harmonization had a positive effect on firms' ability to expand their export volumes, by helping them overcome informational asymmetries. Between 2002 and 2010 exports grew 16 percent faster for products that underwent harmonization than for others. In addition, firms are more likely to introduce new products when regulation for that given product is harmonized. These positive effects are consistent with a reduction in "credibility barriers" in the destination markets. The evidence also suggests that the signaling benefits of harmonization extend across a firm's export portfolio. Exporters are more likely to introduce new products when similar products (within the same HS 2-digit heading) have been harmonized. These results suggest that harmonization positively affects the managerial and production capacity of the firm, in turn facilitating expansion of exports beyond the product concerned.

Next, we explore whether harmonization had an impact on firm profits (measured by the ratio of operating profits to output) and productivity, using the same data on harmonization with data from the Morocco industrial census for the period 1985–2004. Figure 4.8 reports within-firm estimates of the effect of the count of sector-level harmonizations on profits and real labor productivity (see the blue bars labeled "all sectors"). The evidence suggests that the

Box 4.1 Regulatory Harmonization and Firm Performance in Morocco: What Should We Expect?

Morocco has embarked on a process of regulatory convergence toward the EU regulations. This offers an opportunity to examine the different and at times competing channels through which standard harmonization may affect firms' performance.

First, harmonization of NTMs may affect firms' performance through changes in the domestic market structure. In a heterogeneous-firms setting, firms selling domestically must now incur the same regulatory compliance costs as when they export to the European Union (EU). Firms that were already exporting to the EU are not affected directly, since they already had to comply with EU standards. This implies that, while the absolute trade costs between Morocco and the EU do not change, relative costs do. For firms already exporting to the EU, the variable cost of selling domestically goes up as only compliant, high-quality products can be sold following harmonization. For firms that were not already complying with the EU standard—that is the purely domestic sellers, the exporters to other destinations, and the foreign exporters previously exporting to Morocco and non-harmonized markets—the variable costs rise as well, presumably in the same proportion. In addition, they must now incur the sunk and fixed costs of adapting their production lines to the new regulations. The higher fixed costs will induce exit of the least productive firms from the domestic market. This will, in turn, make it more profitable for complying exporters who can now spread the fixed cost over larger exports and domestic sales, but also for EU producers who sell high-quality products in Morocco without facing the competition of low-quality, non-compliant exporters.

Thus, for foreign producers servicing the Moroccan market, two opposite effects are at play:

- A pro-competitive effect akin to trade creation whereby EU producers obtain de facto improved access to the Moroccan market; and
- An anti-competitive effect akin to trade diversion whereby low-quality exporters from developing countries face higher costs to access the Moroccan market.

Which effect dominates is likely to vary across sectors, with the former dominating in sectors initially attractive to EU producers and the latter in sectors initially attractive to developing countries' producers. In itself, the anti-competitive effect would induce Moroccan exporters to redeploy themselves to the domestic market; with a finite elasticity of transformation, this would reduce their export sales to the EU. However, in the presence of economies of scale, their unit costs would be reduced and their export sales could rise.

Second, in addition to these mechanical effects, harmonization can positively impact existing and potential Moroccan exporters through the reduction of informational market failures. Suppose that a Moroccan producer of food containers privately adopts the stringent EU standards and tries to penetrate the EU market claiming that his products are compliant. Given the market's sensitivity, EU packaged food producers are likely to take this claim with skepticism. Now, if the same stringent standards are designed and rigorously enforced in Morocco, such a claim becomes more credible. If this effect is substantial, one would expect a positive effect of harmonization on firms' ability to expand their export at the intensive margin and perhaps even at the extensive margin facilitating the introduction of new products, new destinations, or both.

Source: Compilation based on Augier, Cadot, and Dovis (2014) and Dovis and Jaud (2014).

harmonization of Moroccan regulations on EU standards led to higher profits and labor productivity. The marginal effect of a harmonized NTM is an increase in the average markup rate by 25 percent and an increase in labor-productivity of 23 percent. The effect on productivity may be channeled either through improved efficiency or through capital deepening, as compliance with stiffer standards may have implied the acquisition of new machinery.[4] These results are consistent with the earlier result that harmonizations, although product-specific, have benefits that extend to the firm.

In addition, to this "public-good" dimension, the analysis suggests that regulatory harmonization also has "club-good" effects. Figure 4.8 further reports estimates of the effect of the count of sector-level harmonizations on profits and real labor productivity, separating sectors between those with a high initial share of imports from developing countries and those with a high share of imports from Organisation for Economic Co-operation and Development (OECD) countries. The import share serves as a proxy for sectors in which developing countries and OECD countries, respectively, have a comparative advantage and where the competitive pressure from them is strongest.[5]

Consistent with the "shutting-the-door" effect discussed in box 4.1, figure 4.8 suggests both market-protection (trade-diversion) and entry (trade-creation) effects on profits. Profits are significantly higher in sectors where competition from developing countries is most intense, such as food and beverages and textiles (see figure 4.8). By contrast, in sectors with high import penetration from

Figure 4.8 Did Harmonization Protect Morocco's Home Market?

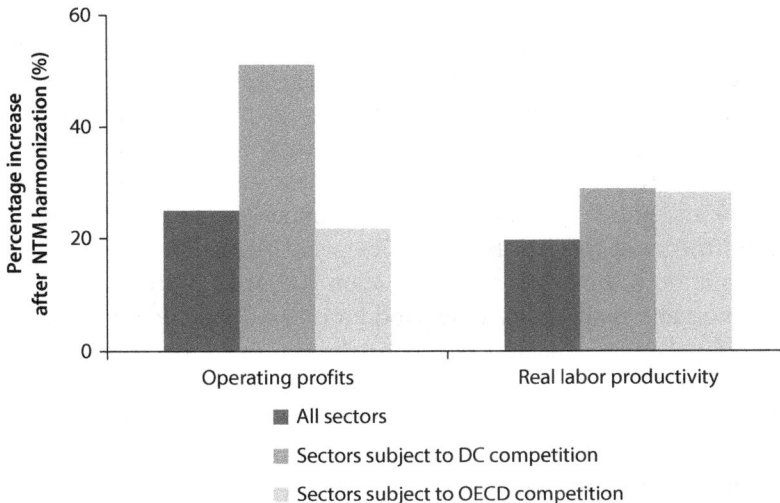

Source: Augier, Cadot, and Dovis 2014.
Note: The figure reports the parameter estimates of the effect of the count of sector-level harmonization on profits and real labor productivity. Each bar corresponds to a different regression. Blue bars report estimates of the effect of harmonization considering all sectors, orange bars considering high DC-penetration sectors and green bars considering high OECD-penetration sectors. All regressions control for firm age, size, and tariffs, and include firm and year fixed-effects. The data are for the 1985–2004 period.

OECD countries, harmonization raises profitability by less or even reduces it, consistent with the pro-competitive effect (see figure 4.8). Thus, harmonization appears to have changed the landscape of the domestic market, by sheltering Moroccan producers from low-cost competition while exposing them to industrial-country competition. On net, the trade-diversion effect seems to dominate. Furthermore, the trade-diversion effect is only temporary. Competitive, low-quality exporters will replace non-complying products with complying ones (probably switching suppliers) within a few years; but those few years may provide a window of relief, like temporary import protection.

Taken together, these results suggest that harmonization on more stringent EU standards, by lowering significantly the costs of exporting to the EU market, by reducing informational asymmetries, and through changes in the level of competition on the domestic market, would have significant and positive effects on Moroccan firms' performance. They also contribute to the political acceptability of costly harmonization. In fact, in most cases regulatory harmonization is done on EU terms, which implies a substantial loss of sovereignty for developing countries. While technical assistance may be provided to help with the convergence process, what really matters is that by harmonizing on stringent standards, Morocco gains some access to the EU markets.

Laissez-Passer: It Matters

In addition to trade costs induced by trade policies, firms' export performances are affected by the cost associated with moving goods across national borders. Trade facilitation is not only about the physical infrastructure for trade—improving poor road or port infrastructure. Administrative hurdles, including numerous customs procedures, tax procedures, clearances, and cargo inspections, impose significant delays, often before the merchandise even reaches port (Djankov, Freund, and Pham 2010). In MENA countries the trade cost associated with arranging export shipments clearing customs are higher than in Asian competitor countries.

Combining Egyptian firm-level export data with data on trade costs from the World Bank's Doing Business report, we examine how trade facilitation affects trade performance at the firm-level. Cumbersome regulations and administrative procedures in both the origin and destination countries depress Egyptian firms' trade volumes and their ability to expand into new destination markets (Hendy and Zaki 2014). Time delays in the origin country have a stronger effect. A 10 percent reduction in the time to export would increase firm export volumes by 1–4 percent—depending on the set of fixed effects used—against 1.3 percent for the time to import. Time delays act as a tax on exports as the exporter needs to incur additional costs associated with the exporting process, storage, and transport of the goods during the delay. Consistent with this, small and medium exporters are also disproportionately more affected by such barriers. Importantly, the effect varies across sectors, with higher-value products depreciating more rapidly. Box 4.2 provides another example of the importance of facilitating firms' access to markets focusing on the West Bank. While the situation in the

West Bank is highly peculiar, the analysis still highlights the importance of removing restrictions to movement of goods and people within and across territories.

Overall, the findings suggest that the success of MENA countries to increase their export growth and diversification as well as create jobs depends heavily on their ability to improve the business climate to facilitate the entry of young, efficient firms and attract productive foreign companies. For this, governments need to significantly reduce trade transaction costs, by streamlining trade facilitation, maintaining open markets, and in particular facilitate efficient sourcing of inputs by eliminating high-tariffs on intermediate imports to help domestic firms' participate in GVC. Modernizing domestic NTMs will also help firms overcome managerial failures and encourage companies to innovate.

Box 4.2 How Valuable Is Market Access? Evidence from the West Bank

The West Bank is a case where the cost of doing business for firms is magnified due to the mobility restrictions imposed by Israel. Such mobility restrictions, including roadblocks, checkpoints, earth mounds, trenches, and a separation barrier wall, are part of the broader "closure" regime instituted by Israel in response to the first Palestinian uprising. Combining data on mobility restrictions in the West Bank with firm-level census and stock-price data, allows estimating the economic costs of barriers to firms' access to (foreign) markets. The analysis makes use of the Mobility Restriction Index (MRI) from (Blankespoor and Van Der Weide 2015). The index compares the population that can be reached within a given time frame under two scenarios, with and without mobility restrictions, and infers from this difference the effective constraints faced by firms in accessing markets.

Map B4.2.1 panel (a) maps the prevalence of mobility restrictions in different localities in the West Bank for 2006 and 2012, with darker dots indicating higher levels of mobility restrictions. The graphs show enormous variation in the prevalence of mobility restrictions both in the cross-section and over time. In parallel panel (b) depicts the density of night time lights, a proxy for economic activity, across the West Bank in 2006 and in 2012. A comparison of the two sets of maps suggests a positive association between the intensity of night time lights and the removal of mobility restrictions, especially in the Northern West Bank where market access was significantly enhanced between 2006 and 2012.

Figure B4.2.1 reports the variation in firms' dynamics (panel a) and profitability proxied by the firms' stock market returns (panel b) against the intensity of mobility restrictions between 2007 and 2012. Gross entry and exit rates tend to be higher in locations that suffer from stronger restrictions to market access. On net, entry rate of firms are significantly lower. Regression analysis estimates that removing restrictions to market access would raise firms' net entry by about 18 percent. Firms are also significantly less profitable in locations where restrictions are the strongest. The estimated impact of existing restrictions on firms' annual stock returns is large; around 27 percent. This implies that the additional cost associated with restrictions impose a toll on firms' profits.

The weaker firm dynamics resulting from mobility restrictions affect economic performance at the aggregate level too (figure B4.2.1, panels c and d). The level of economic activity

box continues next page

Box 4.2 How Valuable Is Market Access? Evidence from the West Bank (continued)

Map B4.2.1 Mobility Restrictions and Night-Time Lights in the West Bank in 2006 and 2012

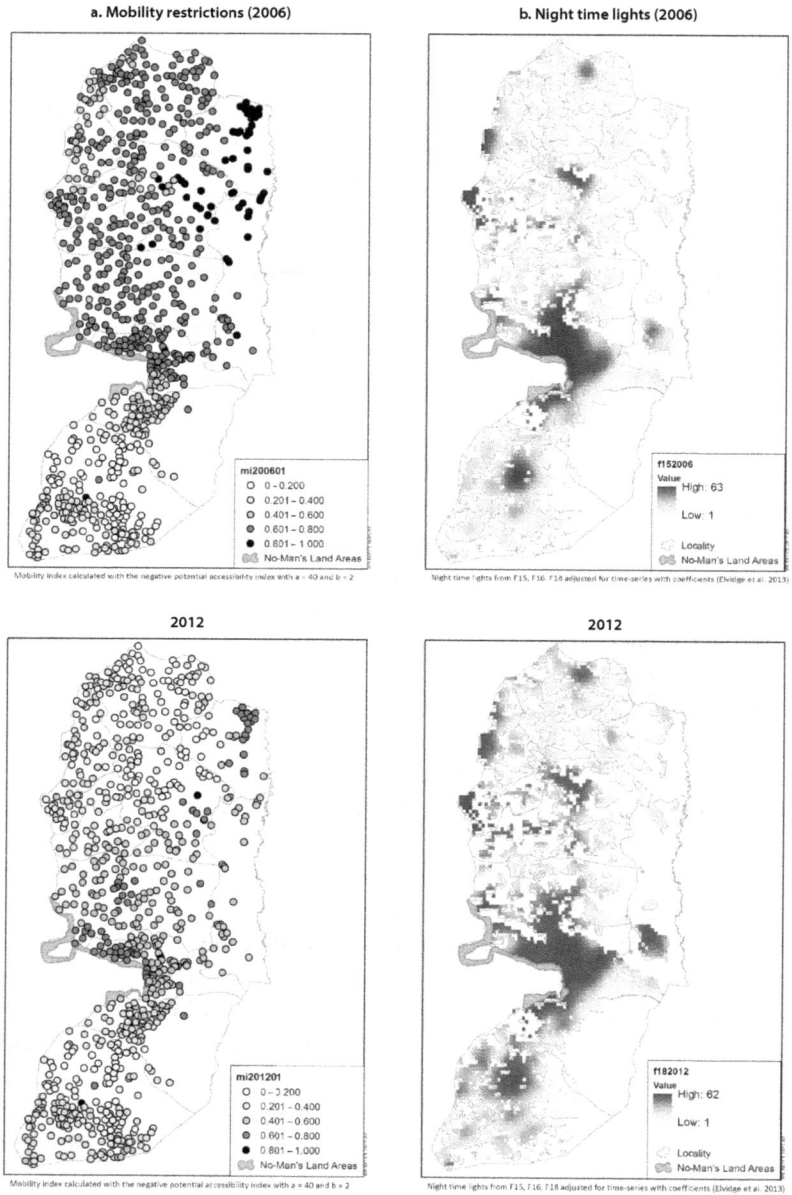

a. Mobility restrictions (2006)

b. Night time lights (2006)

2012

2012

Sources: Elvidge et al. 2013; Blankespoor, Van Der Weide, and Rijkers 2014.
Note: The mobility ratio index is calculated annually for each location in the West Bank.

box continues next page

Box 4.2 How Valuable Is Market Access? Evidence from the West Bank *(continued)*

Figure B4.2.1 Mobility Restrictions and Economic Performance in the West Bank

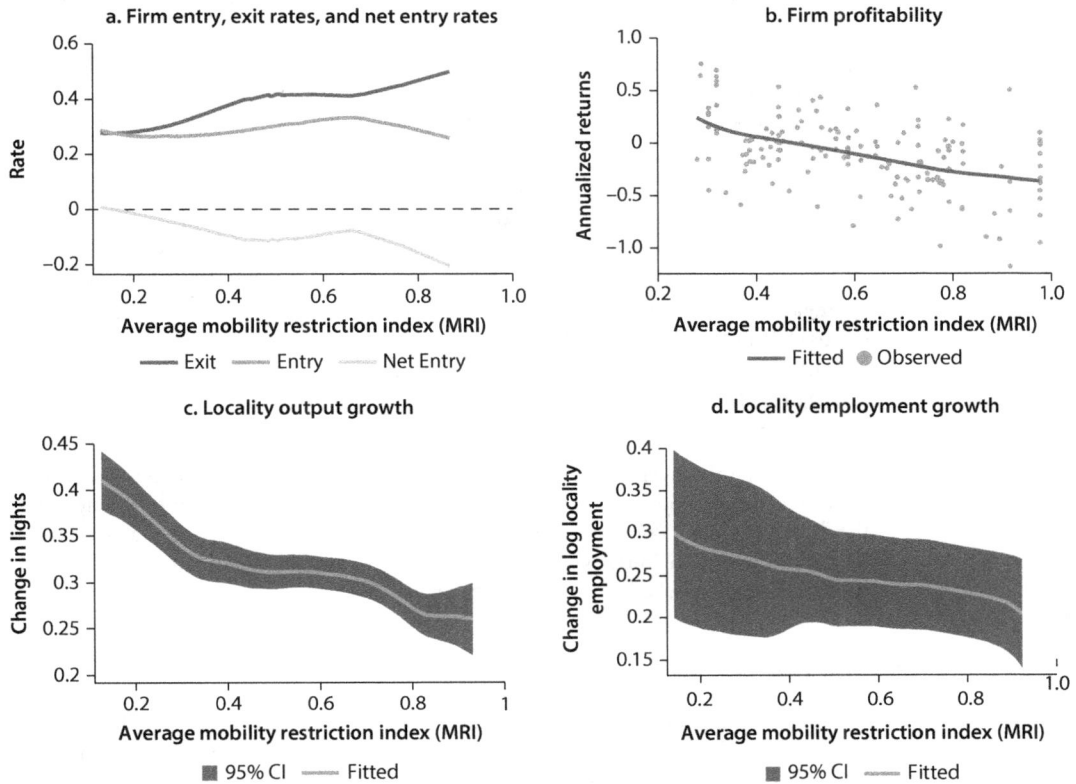

a. Firm entry, exit rates, and net entry rates

— Exit   — Entry   — Net Entry

b. Firm profitability

— Fitted   ● Observed

c. Locality output growth

■ 95% CI   — Fitted

d. Locality employment growth

■ 95% CI   — Fitted

Source: Blankespoor, Van Der Weide, and Rijkers 2014.
Note: Panel (a) reports firm, entry, exit, and net entry rates against average mobility restrictions, and panel (b) plots the log annual stock market returns against average intensity of mobility restrictions. Panel (c) plots the change in night time lights against the average intensity of mobility restrictions over two 4-year periods, 2004–08 and 2008–12. Panel (d) plots the change in locality employment growth against mobility restrictions for the period 2007–12. CI = confidence interval.

at the locality level is measured by night time lights over two 4-year periods, 2004–08 and 2008–12 (panel c). Panel d plots the evolution of employment growth at the locality level against the restriction index. The results suggest that enhanced market access is significantly and positively associated with better economic outcomes. Removing existing restrictions would accelerate local economic growth by approximately 2–6 percentage points each year, a large effect. The impact of restrictions on job growth is negative (panel b), but not always significant.

Taken together, these results suggest that policies that lower the cost of accessing markets for goods and inputs and favor internal movement of labor will trigger a selection process across firms within sectors that will contribute to raising aggregate productivity, output growth, and job creation.

Source: Based on Blankespoor, Van Der Weide, and Rijkers 2014.

Notes

1. The analysis leaves aside the case of quantitative restrictions, as those have largely been phased out, and focus on regulations, either sanitary or technical, of which there is a plethora in high- and middle-income countries.
2. The UN Broad Economic Categories (BEC) focus on the final use of products and distinguish between primary inputs, consumer goods, capital goods, and intermediates. Intermediates correspond to the following categories; 11, 121, 21, 22, 31, 322, 42, 41, 521, 53.
3. Note that this does not completely solve the endogeneity problem. Because imports and exports cannot be matched at the firm-product-destination level but only at the firm level, the individual RCAs are aggregated across products and destinations to generate a firm-level measure of input quality. Weights used in this aggregation are affected by the firm's managerial decisions and are therefore endogenous. Using the average weights for other firms in the same industry rather than weights for the firm itself helps get around this issue. See Le Bris, Disdier, and Jaud (2014) for details.
4. The data does not allow us to observe directly any additional cost, but profits rose.
5. Decomposing the overall harmonization effect between sectors with high penetration from developing countries and OECD countries, respectively, is done by interacting the harmonization count variable with a time-invariant dummy variable marking sectors with a high initial share of imports from developing countries and OECD countries, respectively.

References

Amiti, M., and J. Konings. 2007. "Trade Liberalization, Intermediate Inputs, and Productivity: Evidence from Indonesia." *American Economic Review* 97 (5): 1611–38.

Asprilla, A., N. Berman, O. Cadot, and M. Jaud. 2014. "Pricing-to-Market, Trade Policy, and Market Power." Mimeo.

Augier, P., O. Cadot, and M. Dovis. 2014. "NTM Harmonization, Profits, and Productivity: Firm-Level Evidence from Morocco." Mimeo.

Bas, Maria. 2012. "Input-Trade Liberalization and Firm Export Decisions: Evidence from Argentina." *Journal of Development Economics* 97 (2): 481–93.

Bas, M., and V. Strauss-Kahn. 2011. "Does Importing More Inputs Raise Exports? Firm Level Evidence from France." Working Papers 2011–15, CEPII Research Center.

Bastos, P., J. Silva, and E. Verhoogen. 2013. "Export Destinations and Input Prices: Evidence from Portugal." Manuscript, Columbia University.

Bensassi, S., J. De Sousa, M. Fodha, H. Guimbard, J. Jarreau, E. Milet, D. Mirza, and C. Mitaritonna. 2012. *The Cost of the Non-Mediterranean.* CIREM.

Bernard, A., and B. Jensen. 1995. "Exporters, Jobs and Wages in U.S. Manufacturing, 1976–87." *Brookings Papers on Economic Activity: Microeconomics* 1995: 67–112.

———. 2004. "Why Some Firms Export." *Review of Economics and Statistics* 86: 561–69.

Blankespoor, B., and R. van der Weide. 2015. "Putting a Number to the Restrictions to Mobility in the West Bank." Mimeo.

Blankespoor, B., R. van der Weide, and B. Rijkers. 2014. "How Valuable Is Market Access? Evidence from the West Bank." Mimeo.

Brambilla, I., D. Lederman, and G. Porto. 2012. "Exports, Export Destinations, and Skills." *American Economic Review* 102: 3406–38.

Brander, J., and B. Spencer. 1984. "Tariff Protection and Imperfect Competition." In *Monopolistic Competition and International Trade*, edited by H. Kierzkowski. Oxford, U. K.: Oxford University Press.

Chaney, Thomas. 2013. "Liquidity Constrained Exporters." NBER Working Paper 19170, National Bureau of Economic Research, Boston, MA.

Chevassus-Lozza, E., C. Gaigne, and L. Mener. 2013. "Does Input Trade Liberalization Boost Downstream Firms' Exports? Theory and Firm-Level Evidence." *Journal of International Economics* 90 (2): 391–402.

Cruz, M., and M. Bussolo. 2014. "Does Input Tariff Reduction Impact Firms' Export in the Presence of Import Exemption Regimes?" Mimeo.

Djankov, S., C. Freund, and C. Pham. 2010. "Trading on Time." *Review of Economics and Statistics* 92: 166–73.

Dovis, M., and M. Jaud. 2014. "Standards Harmonization as Export Promotion." Mimeo.

Eaton, J., S. Kortum, and F. Kramarz. 2004. "Dissecting Trade: Firms, Industries, and Export Destinations." *American Economic Review* 94: 150–54.

El-Enbaby, H., R. Hendy, and C. Zaki. 2014. "Do Product Standards Matter for Margins of Trade in Egypt? Evidence from Firm-Level Data." Mimeo.

Elvidge, Christopher D., M. Zhizhin, F-C. Hsu, and K. E. Baugh. 2013. "VIIRS Nightfire: Satellite Pyrometry at Night." Remote Sens. 5, no. 9: 4423–49.

Feng, L., Z. Li, and D. Swenson. 2012. "The Connection between Imported Intermediate Inputs and Exports: Evidence from Chinese Firms." NBER Working Papers 18260, National Bureau of Economic Research, Boston, MA.

Fontagné, L., G. Orefice, R. Piermartini, and N. Rocha. 2013. "Product Standards and Margins of Trade: Firm Level Evidence." CEPII Research Center, Paris.

Frías, J., D. Kaplan, and E. Verhoogen. 2012. "Exports and Wage Premia: Evidence from Mexican Employer-Employee Data." *American Economic Review Papers & Proceedings* 102: 435–40.

Goldberg, P. K., A. K. Khandelwal, N. Pavcnik, and P. Topalova. 2010. "Imported Intermediate Inputs and Domestic Product Growth: Evidence from India." *The Quarterly Journal of Economics* 125 (4): 1727–67.

Hendy, R., and C. Zaki. 2014. "Trade Facilitation and Firms Exports: The Case of Egypt." Mimeo.

Javorcik, Beata Smarzynska. 2004. "Does Foreign Direct Investment Increase the Productivity of Domestic Firms? In Search of Spillovers through Backward Linkages." *American Economic Review* 94 (3): 605–27.

Kasahara, H., and J. Rodrigue. 2008. "Does the Use of Imported Intermediates Increase Productivity? Plant-Level Evidence." *Journal of Development Economics* 87: 106–18.

Kee, Hiau Looi. 2015. "Local Intermediate Inputs and the Shared Supplier Spillovers of Foreign Direct Investment." *Journal of Development Economics* 112: 56–71.

Kee, H. L., and H. Tang. 2012. "Domestic Value Added in Chinese Exports: Firm-level Evidence." World Bank.

Kugler, Maurice. 2006. "Spillovers from Foreign Direct Investment: Within or between Industries?" *Journal of Development Economics* 80 (2): 444–77.

Le Bris, F., A. C. Disdier, and M. Jaud. 2014. "Boosting Exports through Intermediate Input Imports?" Mimeo.

Manova, K., and Z. Zhang. 2012. "Export Prices across Firms and Destinations." *Quarterly Journal of Economics* 127: 379–436.

Melitz, Marc J. 2003. "The Impact of Trade on Intra-Industry Reallocations and Aggregate Industry Productivity." *Econometrica* 71: 1695–725.

Rijkers, Bob, C. Freund and A. Nucifora. 2014. "All in the Family: State Capture in Tunisia," Policy Research Working Paper Series 6810, World Bank.

Rouis, M., and S. Tabor. 2013. *Regional Economic Integration in the Middle East and North Africa: Beyond Trade Reforms*. Washington, DC: World Bank.

World Bank. 2009. *From Privilege to Competition: Unlocking Private-Led Growth in the Middle East and North Africa*. Washington, DC: World Bank.

———. 2013. *Boosting Competition in the Tunisian Markets: A Policy Approach to Opening Markets to New Investment and Employment Opportunities*. World Bank, Washington, DC.

———. 2014. *Jobs or Privileges: Unleashing the Employment Potential of the Middle East and North Africa*. Washington, DC: World Bank.

Wood, C., and J. Yang. 2014. "Export Performance and Specialization—The Role of Financial Sector Development and Governance in MENA." Mimeo.

CHAPTER 5

Industrial Policy in MENA: The Small and the Big

Key Messages

After two decades of unenthusiastic application of the Washington consensus, industrial policy is coming back into fashion in Middle East and North Africa (MENA). Is industrial policy the answer to MENA's weak export performance? In spite of decades of debate, evidence on whether industrial policy works or not still relies very much on qualitative assessments. In this chapter we rely on firm-level analysis to assess the record of policy intervention in MENA and go beyond the anecdotes. MENA's prevalent cronyism and corruption under pre-Arab Spring regimes led to distortionary allocation of favors and rent dissipation by beneficiary firms, with little evidence that those firms developed into national champions. In contrast, some forms of clinical intervention, like export promotion, seem to work. However, the effects apply primarily to small firms that are a tiny fraction of aggregate exports and cannot address key weaknesses at the top. In other words, ground-level policies may work, but they are not game-changers.

Export Promotion: Too Small to Matter

One strand of the literature argues that firms' ability to export comes from firms' improved productivity through accumulated experience on the domestic market (see Clerides, Lach, and Tybout 1998 for Morocco; see also Bernard and Jensen 1999a, 1999b, or Bigsten et al. 2000). If there is no "learning by exporting," the domestic market acts as a breeding ground for future exporters by being both sufficiently protected to ensure survival and sufficiently competitive to encourage innovation and efficiency, leaving little scope for useful assistance. By contrast, a second strand of the literature provides evidence that firms learn how to export not only from improved productivity but also from improved familiarity with foreign markets (Aw, Chung, and Roberts 2000). In Morocco, young firms are more likely to export than older ones and 42 percent of firms start exporting in the year of their creation (Fafchamps, el Hamine, and Zeufack 2002).

These short transitions into exporting do not support the view that firms need to improve productivity prior to exporting. Furthermore, 80 percent of exported products were exported the first year they were produced by firms, suggesting they were designed for export from the start (Fafchamps, el Hamine, and Zeufack 2002).

In addition, exporting typically involves uncertainty; it is by trial and error that individual entrepreneurs discover what they can profitably export. While this search takes place at the firm level, it generates information that has value beyond its boundaries, as export success at the product-destination level is imitable. This informational externality is not corrected by any institutional mechanism comparable to patents for product innovation. As a result, export entrepreneurship has the characteristics of a public good and is under-supplied in equilibrium, further justifying government support (Hausmann and Rodrik 2003).

Many developing countries including in MENA rest their export strategies on national export promotion agencies whose job is to help firms overcome the cost and risks associated with entering new foreign markets. Cross-country evidence suggests that export-promotion agencies (EPAs), on average, have a large and significant effect on export growth (Lederman, Olarreaga, and Payton 2010). They are also important for export diversification (Zoratto 2013). As usual in cross-country studies, the very large size of the coefficient suggests that it captures some confounding influences as well. Table 5.1 shows that most EPAs in MENA are relatively new, created in the late 1990s and early 2000s, with the exception of the Israeli and Tunisian agencies.

In terms of the size of their budget, EPAs in MENA region rank at the 4th place with 0.18 percent of annual exports spent on export promotion, behind Sub-Saharan Africa with 0.34 percent, Latin America and the Caribbean with 0.21 percent, and Eastern Europe and Asia with 0.19 percent (see figure 5.1).

Table 5.1 Export-Promotion Agencies in MENA

Economy	Agency name	Date of creation
Algeria	ALGEX	1997
Egypt, Arab Rep.	EPCC	1997
Israel	Israel Export International Cooperation Institute	1958
Jordan	JEDCO	2003
Lebanon	IDAL	1994
Malta	Malta Enterprise	2004
Morocco	CMPE	1981
Oman	OCIPED	1996
West Bank	Paltrade	1999
Syrian Arab Republic	EDPA	2009
Tunisia	CEPEX	1973
Yemen, Rep.	Yemen Export Supreme Council	1997

Source: Olarreaga and Zoratto 2014.
Note: Data are from the 2010 World Bank Export Promotion Agencies Survey.

Figure 5.1 Regional Export-Promotion Agencies' Expenditure over Exports

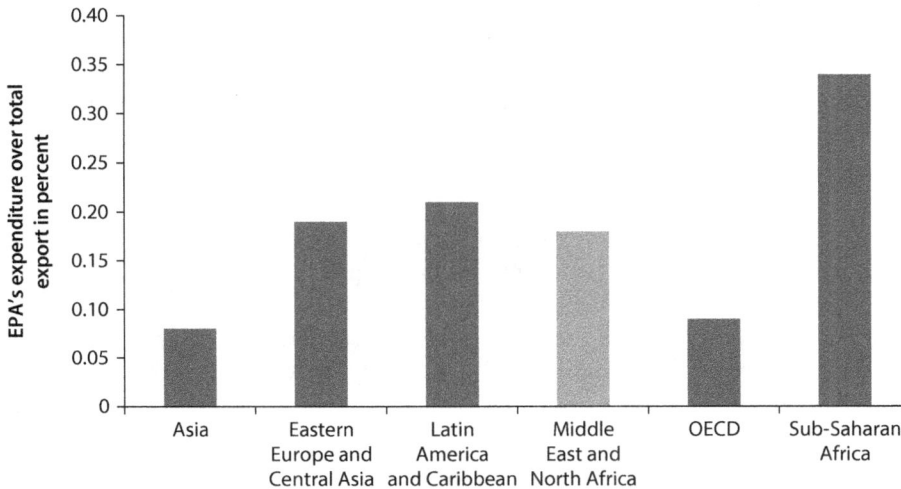

Source: Olarreaga and Zoratto 2014.
Note: Data are from the 2010 World Bank Export Promotion Agencies Survey.

In addition, a breakdown of export promotion strategies by region reveals that, on average, EPAs in the MENA region emphasize diversification of export products relatively more than EPAs in other regions. Like other EPAs, those in MENA target small exporters, reflecting the belief that small firms are primary sources of job creation. However, the evidence reported in this study suggests that export growth takes place more toward the top of the distribution, which is generally unattended by EPAs. Thus, even if such interventions have positive effects on small exporters, the aggregate impact may be limited, because those firms can only contribute a small amount in total exports.

At the micro level, several trade-related support programs implemented in MENA countries have been subject to rigorous impact evaluation. In Tunisia, using combined information, the export-promotion program, FAMEX, with firm trade and census data, Cadot et al. (2015), find that the FAMEX had a non-negligible effect on export performance at the firm level. They estimate a 50 percent impact on export sales compared to a control group. However, the effect on export sales proved to be transient: Three years after the intervention, beneficiaries' export sales were not significantly different from those of the control group. Yet, even a transient effect generates gains, estimated at about nine dollars of additional exports for a dollar of support. The lack of strong evidence of spillovers from treated to non-treated firms limits the justification for the program's "grant" dimension. This is further compounded by FAMEX's questionable additional objective of encouraging the growth of the domestic export-consulting sector, considering Ben Ali cronies were particularly active in consulting. Experience from Jordan, with the government export-promotion program (JEDCO) and a production capacity upgrading program (JUMP), suggests similar results. In addition to raising firms' exports, both programs had a positive impact on job creation (Fernandes, Gourdon, and Jaud 2014).

Overall the new evidence suggests that using government funds to address a genuine issue, namely the difficulty for firms to gain information about export markets, could help boost MENA firms' exports (see box 5.1). In addition, export promotion is one of the few areas of industrial policy that has been subjected to rigorous impact evaluation. These findings also help advance our understanding of what works and thus improve the choice and design of policies to effectively increase private sector development and export growth.

Given the positive impact of government interventions, why is it that on aggregate, MENA's exports have not grown faster? The reason is in part due to the fact that export strategies in MENA countries tend to be centered on small and medium enterprises (SMEs). In this section we show why this emphasis was

---

Box 5.1 Export Support: Remedy or Addictive Drug?

One of the objectives of Tunisia's FAMEX was to help small exporters "grow out" of single-buyer subcontracting relationships. For example, the owner of a small firm employing nine female workers in Sousse, Tunisia, used to make lingerie for a Belgian client who provided the inputs and paid the owner a fee. When asked, as part of a survey, why she did not prospect other clients abroad to produce independently, she responded, "I am afraid to do it, because my sole client may learn about it, and I may lose him. You understand, I would need to invest a lot upfront in market research, travel abroad, and so on. Also, there is no one with expertise in Tunisia who could help me overcome these knowledge gaps. The upfront investment is just too high for me when I am very uncertain about the outcome. I just cannot afford it."

At the same time, the survey also highlighted an unwanted side effect of government assistance. Another Tunisian garment producer had a French designer come to his premises for two months to design his Ladies Spring collection for export to Italy and France. The designer's trip expenses and fees, about $60,000, were covered by a government program. The firm's owner had an unsurprisingly positive view of government intervention: "Overall, the business environment is good in Tunisia. The government supports the industry, as it did for the design of my Spring collection. My problem is that we can only benefit from that program once. What am I going to do for the coming Fall collection? This is a problem. The government should change its program and allow us to benefit from it more often." As the World Bank (2009) study concludes, "This kind of dependence characterizes many private firms across the region. It is typical of many MENA entrepreneurs who grow accustomed to state protection and support. Indeed, 'additional government support and protection' is the dominant advocacy line of many business associations in the region."

Source: World Bank 2009.

---

misguided. In addition we show that the specificities of the distribution of exporters in MENA countries can help us assess the records of government interventions in MENA.

The dominance of large firms on export volumes and export growth implies that for aggregate, exports to grow, the top 1 percent of firms needs to grow, or new firms need to become superstars. Research suggests that it is extremely rare for a small exporter to grow gradually and join the top 1 percent in a decade, even in poor countries (Freund and Pierola forthcoming). Either firms in the top 1 percent were already superstars 10 years earlier, or they grew rapidly, in about three years, to become ones. In MENA countries, Morocco is the only country where there is enough data to examine the dynamics among superstars over the past decade. The results suggest that there is indeed less dynamism at the top of the distribution as compared with two Latin American countries, Costa Rica and Peru. Over 50 percent of today's superstars in Morocco were already superstars 10 years earlier. This is significantly more than in Costa Rica (30 percent) and Peru (36 percent), where more churning may explain the overall better performance of the top group. Those results may partly reflect the proximity to the European Union's (EU) tough export markets, which set the bar high for entry and survival of MENA firms in terms of productivity and quality. They also most likely reflect the unfriendly business climate, including cumbersome regulations and constraints on the availability of key factors, that prevails in MENA countries (see chapter 4), making it difficult for top firms to expand and even more difficult for young firms to thrive to the top. Thus, these results imply that directing resources to the average SME will do little to spur export growth.

In MENA as elsewhere, governments intervene to help SMEs enter the export market, by lowering entry costs or offering subsidized resources. The rationale is that SMEs suffer relatively more from market failures and that if helped they could contribute significantly to both exports and job creation. As to their contribution to exports, if SMEs in MENA are small because they are typically among the least efficient producers and can produce only small quantities, then, even if government interventions help them enter the export market, their exports are likely to be so small that their effect on aggregate exports will be marginal. However, if indeed SMEs in MENA are small because of distortions that prevent them from growing to be large firms, then policies that help eliminate such distortions may have important aggregate effects.

As a jobs strategy, the SME focus in MENA is also misguided. While SMEs are often perceived to create more jobs than large, declining firms, they also destroy the most jobs. Recent evidence shows that in the United States, what accounts for higher-than-average rates of job creation at the firm level is not smallness but young age (Haltiwanger, Jarmin, and Miranda 2011). Young (newly created) firms create jobs while they grow, but some firms stay small and those do not create more jobs than larger ones. Put differently, when age is controlled for, size is no longer significant as a driver of firm-level job creation. In MENA, Enterprise Surveys data, suggest that firms tend to be older than elsewhere

(World Bank 2009). More recent evidence shows that the net employment creation is dominated by young startups, the "gazelles" that do grow rapidly into large firms, and young large firms (World Bank 2013, 2014). These results help explain the persistently-small impact of SME support programs on aggregate employment and export growth.

Finally, since sector-level industrial policies typically target the top-end of the market, providing packages of incentives to foreign companies, the performance of the top 1 percent of exporters can tell us something about the record of industrial policy in MENA. In MENA while the single largest firm tends to be relatively large as compared with other countries' firms, the other top 1 percent firms are not as outstanding performers. This is surprising, as the objective of industrial policy is to create "national champions" with sufficient scale and scope to establish themselves in international markets. In this respect, the results suggest that industrial policy in MENA seems to have failed to nurture a group of "world class" exporters in comparative-advantage sectors capable of lifting its export performance.

Taken together these results suggest that in MENA instead of intervention focusing on SMEs, what is needed is a broad package to expand incentives for exporting by the most efficient and innovative firms that drive export growth and net job creation. In the next section we discuss the disproportionate importance of the top firm and how this could relate to the region's political economy.

Champions or Cronies?

While the firm-level evidence discussed in the previous section suggests that industrial policy in MENA has not succeeded in creating the strong fabric of "export superstars" that could drive aggregate export expansion, the disproportionate importance of the top firm raises questions about the targeting of favors towards particular firms. Raymond Fisman's seminal work on the stock market's reaction to rumors about the health of Indonesia's president Suharto revealed the value of political connections at the firm level. A similar exercise on Egyptian firms following the fall of Mubarak's regime in 2012 found that just 20 politically-connected groups accounted for half of the Egyptian stock market's valuation before the regime's fall (Chekir and Diwan 2013). The valuation of these groups grew rapidly in the regime's twilight years, their median value growing from 50 percent more than that of other firms in 2002 to seven in 2010. These groups were mostly present in two non-tradable sectors, construction and services, and two tradable sectors, textiles and metals, although they were essentially serving the domestic market. The regime's fall was associated with an average stock-price loss of 31 percent for those firms, compared to 16 percent for others, even after controlling for sector fixed effects. This effect, applied on a combined stock market valuation of about $30 billion in 2010, brings the value of political connections in the

Arab Republic of Egypt—the present discounted value of excess profits—to a hefty $4.5 billion. Interestingly, the return on equity for those firms was larger, reflecting privileges in their ability to borrow (their debt-to-equity ratios where higher than those of other firms), but the return on assets was lower by about 2 percent. This result is consistent with that obtained on a worldwide panel of politically connected firms (Faccio 2006, 2010). Bertrand et al. (2007) found a similar result for French firms and explained it by showing that politically connected firms tended to over-hire. For instance, they were slightly less likely than non-connected firms to close a plant during a tight-race municipal-election campaign. The evidence implies, therefore, that political favors tend to come with reciprocal obligations, but that the net effect on market valuation is positive.

Tunisia's Jasmin revolution offered a unique opportunity to assess the extent of the Ben Ali (BA) family's stranglehold on the country's economy (Rijkers, Freund, and Nucifora 2014). Combining the Confiscation Commission's list of about 300 firms linked to the BA family with census and Finance Ministry data reveals that BA firms controlled 39 percent of the industry turnover in telecoms, 15 percent in automobile trade, 9 percent in transport, and 3.6 percent in real estate and consulting. Those sectors are essentially nontradables, sheltered from international competition and certainly from the discipline of export markets. The heavy presence of BA firms in real estate also puts in perspective the development of the country's tourism sector and the decades of government promotion and assistance through tax holidays for new hotels, loans at subsidized interest rates for tourism investments, preferred access to land, and direct subsidies (see Nabli et al. 2006). BA firms chose sectors protected by entry and foreign direct investment (FDI) restrictions, as well as fiscal advantages. However, a regression of profits on firm and sector characteristics returns a negative coefficient on the BA dummy, suggesting either poor management or, in accordance with the international evidence discussed above, reciprocating favors such as over-employment. There is also evidence that sectors with high regulatory barriers (entry/FDI restrictions and selective fiscal incentives) underperformed; however, in those sectors, those restrictions were manipulated to benefit BA firms.

A related question is whether BA firms selected into protected industries or whether regulations proliferated in sectors where they would benefit disproportionately more BA firms. The data used do not allow us to formally assess the direction of causation beyond the joint determination of regulation and entry decisions. Only a replication over several countries would reveal if crony-firm entry and regulatory capture follow idiosyncratic patterns—for instance the business history of the ruling family—or, on the contrary, if some sectors are intrinsically prone to regulatory capture—because entry is easily regulated and potential monopoly profits are high.

Studies of politically-connected firms in France found that they did not benefit from over-generous tax treatment (Bertrand et al. 2007), and even in the heavily corrupt environment of Mubarak's Egypt, Chekir and Diwan (2013) find no evidence of favorable tax treatment. In Tunisia, however, 50 importing firms linked to the BA family and confiscated after the regime's fall, were found to have apparently engaged in tariff evasion on a large scale (Rijkers, Raballand, and Baghdadi 2014). This is shown by the increased discrepancies between unit values on the export and import side in sectors where such firms are present. Moreover, anecdotal evidence suggests that some of those firms were using the duty suspension regime for temporary imports even though they were not exporting.[1] Thus, even basic State functions like tax collection were negatively affected by favoritism, as is often the case in the worst governance environments.

In sum, MENA's extensive experience with cronyism under the pre-Arab Spring regimes confirms that business-government ties led to distortionary allocation of favors and rent dissipation by beneficiary firms, with little evidence that those firms developed into national champions or helped lift the region's export performance. However, the literature suggests little in the way of causation between industrial policy and cronyism. Corruption was pervasive in all aspects of government action, even the most "horizontal" ones—Leila Ben Ali had one of Tunisia's most respected schools closed to eliminate competition for a school she had launched—and not just in targeted industry-promotion plans. In fact, there is little overlap between the sectors of predilection of politically-connected firms (largely nontradable sectors sheltered from competition), and the open sectors where companies benefiting from the limited incentives of sectoral policy operated. But these nontradable sectors, because their prices were high, made it harder for the tradable sectors (that used their outputs as inputs) to compete in world markets.

A follow-up question is whether the relative larger size of the top single exporters in MENA may be due to these firms being cronies. While the customs data does not allow us to answer this question for all MENA countries, in the case of Tunisia this is unlikely to be the case, as most crony firms were located in non-tradable sectors. Things might have been different in Egypt under Mubarak. In Morocco and Jordan, where systematic research was done on the few very large top firms, results suggest that most of those large companies are foreign-owned and are therefore unlikely to be crony-firms.

Note

1. This regime was meant for inputs that would be processed into products for export.

References

Aw, B. Y., S. Chung, and M. Roberts. 2000. "Productivity and Turnover in the Export Market: Micro-level Evidence from the Republic of Korea and Taiwan." *World Bank Economic Review* 14: 65–90.

Bernard, A., and B. Jensen. 1999a. "Exception Exporter Performance: Cause, Effect, or Both?" *Journal of International Economics* 47: 1–25.

———. 1999b. "Exporting and Productivity." NBER Working Paper 7135, National Bureau of Economic Research, Boston, MA.

Bertrand, M., F. Kramarz, A. Schoar, and D. Thesmar. 2007. *Politicians, Firms, and the Political Business Cycle: Evidence from France.* PSE/University of Chicago.

Bigsten, Arne. et al. 2000. *Exports and Firm-level Efficiency in the African Manufacturing Sector.* Mimeo.

Cadot, O., A. M. Fernandes, J. Gourdon, and A. Mattoo. 2015. "Are the Benefits of Export Support Durable? Evidence from Tunisia." WPS 6295.

Chekir, H., and I. Diwan. 2013. "Crony Capitalism in Egypt." Center for International Development Working Paper 250, Harvard University, Cambridge, MA.

Clerides, S., S. Lach, and J. Tybout. 1998. "Is Learning-By-Exporting Important? Micro-Dynamic Evidence from Colombia, Mexico, and Morocco." *Quarterly Journal of Economics* 113: 903–47.

Crawford, Robert. 2013. "Kindi: A Case Study." Columbia Global Centers, New York.

Faccio, Mara. 2006. "Politically-Connected Firms." *American Economic Review* 96: 369–86.

———. 2010. "Differences between Politically Connected and Nonconnected Firms: A Cross-Country Analysis." *Financial Management* 39: 905–28.

Fafchamps, M., S. el Hamine, and A. Zeufack. 2002. "Learning to Export: Evidence from Moroccan Manufacturing." Oxford/ World Bank.

Fernandes, A., J. Gourdon, and M. Jaud. 2014. "Evaluating the Effect of Jordan's Export-Promotion Program." World Bank.

Fisman, Raymond. 2001. "Estimating the Value of Political Connections." *American Economic Review* 91: 1095–102.

Freund, C., and M. Pierola. Forthcoming. "Export Superstars." *The Review of Economics and Statistics.*

Haltiwanger, J., R. Jarmin, and J. Miranda. 2011. "Who Creates Jobs? Small vs Large vs Young." University of Maryland.

Hausmann, R., and D. Rodrik. 2003. "Economic Development as Self-Discovery." *Journal of Development Economics* 72: 603–33.

Lederman, D., M. Olarreaga, and L. Payton. 2010. "Export Promotion Agencies: Do they Work?" *Journal of Development Economics* 91: 257–65.

Nabli, M., J. Keller, C. Nassif, and C. Silva-Jauregui. 2006. "The Political Economy of Industrial Policy in the Middle East and North Africa." World Bank.

Olarreaga, M., and L. Zoratto. 2014. "Export Promotion in the Middle East and North Africa." Mimeo.

Rijkers, B., C. Freund, and A. Nucifora. 2014. "All in the Family: State Capture in Tunisia." Policy Research Working Paper Series 6810, World Bank.

Rijkers, B., G. Raballand, and L. Baghdadi. 2014. "Political Connections and Tariff Evasion: Evidence from Tunisia." Mimeo.

Taglioni, D., and D. Winkler. 2014. "Morocco: Sustaining Economic Growth through Trade." World Bank.

World Bank. 2009. *From Privilege to Competition: Unlocking Private-Led Growth in the Middle East and North Africa.* Washington, DC: World Bank.

———. 2013. *Boosting Competition in the Tunisian Markets: A Policy Approach to Opening Markets to New Investment and Employment Opportunities.* Washington, DC: World Bank.

———. 2014. *Jobs or Privileges: Unleashing the Employment Potential of the Middle East and North Africa.* Washington, DC: World Bank.

Zoratto, L. 2013. *Trade Policy and Export Diversification.* Graduate Institute of International and Development Studies, Geneva.

CHAPTER 6

Building Export Champions: Implications for Policy

MENA Needs More Export Champions

Traditional discussions of export performance are typically cast in terms of countries and sectors—which has a comparative advantage, what should be protected, and so on. Yet, neither countries nor sectors trade; firms do. By exploiting a rich, firm-level data set on exporters in the Middle East and North Africa (MENA), this report sheds new evidence on a number of old questions—ranging from the effects of exchange rate policy to market structure to export promotion to industrial policy—where a firm-level perspective makes it possible to move beyond well-worn diagnoses and debates. While the findings in this report have implications beyond MENA, they have particular salience to the region where job creation and economic growth have never been more urgent.

Based on the new data, evidence reported in this report provides new perspectives on how policy affects trade costs and market structure. Carrying out the analysis at the level of the firm makes it possible to identify these effects through largely unexplored adjustment margins like pricing or the breadth of product and destination portfolios. Moreover, the very fine level of disaggregation of the data allows us to estimate for "within-firm" effects, filtering out many confounding influences. This improves substantially the quality of inference and allows for more robust evaluation of policy impacts and ultimately policy prescriptions.

The central finding is that the size distribution of MENA's exporting firms is suggestive of a critical weakness at the top. Chapter 2 shows that MENA has champions (the individual firms at the top of the distributions) of a size comparable to other regions, but it lacks teams of world-class exporters to surround and emulate the "number ones." Its top 1 percent exporters are significantly smaller, on average, than in other regions. Thus, in MENA the largest exporter is alone at the top—Zidane without a team. In addition, top exporters in MENA do not seem to drive comparative advantage at the country level as is typically found in other regions. These results suggest that MENA champions may lack the right environment and incentives to thrive. They may also suggest that large-firm strategies reflect, at least partly, a legacy of distorted incentives.

Part of the problem is the lack of a competitive real exchange rate. Chapter 3 shows how the deleterious effects of an uncompetitive currency can be traced all the way down to the level of the firm, hurting expansion at the intensive and extensive margin and preventing the emergence of export take-offs. The lack of heavy weight exporters at the top of the distribution also reflects the region's failure to push for trade and business climate reforms energetically. Chapter 4 shows that in an already competition-deficient environment, higher-than-average tariffs and restrictive non-tariff measures (NTMs) have further reduced domestic competition and thus export competitiveness. The high tariffs on intermediate products have also hampered firms' productivity and export growth. In addition, contrary to widely-held views, regulatory modernization can help domestic firms overcome managerial failures and upgrade quality, in turn raising their performance. The costs of MENA's failure to develop effective export champions are potentially high in view of the region's acute job problem. Exporting firms do create more and better jobs. Thus, providing them with the right enabling environment is the region's key policy challenge.

In MENA as elsewhere, sluggish export performance makes it tempting for governments to try industrial policy. Chapter 5 documents how MENA's prevalent cronyism and corruption under pre-Arab Spring regimes led to distortionary allocation of favors and rent dissipation by beneficiary firms, with little evidence that those firms developed into national champions or helped lift the region's export performance. This in itself should call for caution when advocating any form of government intervention. In contrast, while the potential for capture and government failures is large, some interventions, like export promotion, seem to work. However, the effects apply primarily to small firms that contribute little to aggregate exports and cannot address key weaknesses at the top. In other words, ground-level policies may work, but they are not game-changers.

Some Policy Leads

Taken together, the findings in the report suggest that the success of MENA countries to promote export growth and diversification as well as create jobs depends heavily on their ability to create an environment where large firms can invest and expand exports and new efficient firms can thrive to the top.

A number of policy options are likely to help achieve this objective:

1. Governments in MENA should seek a competitive real exchange rate that will help firms grow and gain access to new markets. MENA exchange rate regimes are still predominantly pegged regimes. In a world where MENA exporters are faced with Chinese and other Asian price competitors, with currencies significantly undervalued against the dollar, the exchange rate cannot be ignored in a strategy to boost exporters' competitiveness. How could MENA countries move to more flexible exchange rate regimes? Until now,

any exchange-rate adjustment was difficult to manage fiscally because of the prevalence of energy subsidies. Eliminating subsidies especially now that energy prices are at an historical low is a first step in adjusting the exchange rate to more competitive levels.

2. Governments in MENA need to make significant strides in improving the business climate to facilitate the entry of young, efficient firms and attract productive foreign companies. For this, governments need to significantly reduce trade costs, by improving the quality of infrastructure, improving trade logistics and streamlining export procedures. Eliminating restrictions on the internal movement of labor and goods will also help raise firms' productivity and hence competitiveness. Governments also need to push trade reforms more energetically. Closing MENA markets to competition with high tariffs and restrictive NTMs has not helped domestic exporters grow. The region's governments need to facilitate efficient sourcing of inputs by eliminating high-tariffs on intermediate imports to help domestic firms' participate in global value chains (GVC). Modernizing domestic NTMs will also help firms overcome managerial failures and encourage companies to innovate. Publicizing the domestic enforcement of high norms as a quality-signaling strategy may also help expand the constituency in favor of more regulatory convergence.

3. Attracting foreign direct investment (FDI) has particular importance in the development of effective export champions. Superstars typically enter the export market when they are relatively large, often through foreign invest-ment, and reach the top 1 percent within a few years of exporting. This highlights the role of multinationals in exports. Furthermore, the entry of new large exporters will expand competitive pressure on incumbents and boost overall performance. In MENA, the weaker performance and life-cycle dynamics of the top 1 percent could reflect lower levels of competition from foreign companies resulting from lower flows of FDI going to the region. Thus, policies to attract large, productive multinational firms are likely to be crucial for MENA countries' exports and diversification. As foreign companies tend to pay higher wages, FDI would contribute to the job agenda too. Importantly, given the region's track record, there is a very real concern that attempts to facilitate the emergence of export champions may be captured and tailored to a few, favored firms rather than enable the entry or growth of young produc-tive ones.

4. Finally, if the goal is to increase exports and diversification, MENA govern-ments may need to rethink their approach to export promotion. The fact that very few large firms make up the bulk of exports implies that entry costs are relatively less important than variable trade costs for promoting aggregate exports. Policies that disproportionately allocate resources to help small and medium enterprises (SMEs) enter the export market, by lowering entry costs or offering subsidized resources, are unlikely, even if they work, to translate into economically meaningful aggregate effects—since these firms are too small to matter. Only, if SMEs in MENA are small because of distortions that

prevent them from growing to be large firms, could policies that help eliminate such distortions have important aggregate effects. But their focus needs to be on removing distortions not promoting specific firms.

Many of these policy recommendations are the types of reforms that development institutions, such as the World Bank, have been advising countries in MENA to implement over the past decade. The difference this time is that the firm-level evidence in this report allows MENA governments to better quantify the costs, in terms of forgone trade and jobs, of not having moved ahead more rapidly on such reforms.

Firm-Level Data and Competitiveness Indicators

Firm-Level Data

The analysis builds on a unique dataset that contains information on non-oil export transactions by firm, product (HS 6-digit), and destination in eight MENA countries—the Arab Republic of Egypt, the Islamic Republic of Iran, Jordan, Kuwait, Lebanon, Morocco, Tunisia, and the Republic of Yemen. The data cover all firms that export non-oil products (Harmonized System chapters 01 to 97 excluding HS chapter 27). The data are available over a sample period that varies between 3 years (Kuwait) and 10 years (Tunisia and Morocco) but that mostly cover the years 2004 onwards. The data have been gathered for the use of the report in collaboration with the Economic Research Forum under the Open Access Micro Data Initiative (OAMDI) and is part of the larger World Bank Exporter Dynamics Database (EDD), an ongoing data-collection project that has gathered firm-level transactions data from 45 countries, of which 37 are developing ones (Cebeci et al. 2012).[1] In most cases, the data have been collected directly from Customs authorities, Ministries of Finance or Commerce, and National Statistics Institutes. In other instances, the data have been collected indirectly through local economic institutions (Egypt) or purchased from a private company based on inputs from customs authorities (Chile, Colombia, and Ecuador). In the case of Tunisia, the firm-level data is only accessible in the Institut National de la Statistique (INS) in Tunis, for this reason EDD indicators could not be computed and Tunisia is not included in the EDD.

Two limitations of the data should be noted. First, as the source is customs, we are constrained to focus on trade in goods only. Second, the dataset is very large (several million observations) but contains few covariates as customs data are not systematically reconciled with manufacturing census data. Therefore all we know about exporting firms is their export transactions; other firm characteristics such as overall sales, employment, and balance-sheet information are not available. In the case of Tunisia we were able to obtain the exporter-level transactions data merged with the industrial census data and confidential tax data, giving us access to key firm characteristics such as employment, profits, gross output per worker and wages. In the case of the West Bank, we rely on the firm-level census data merged with stock prices data.

Table A.1 provides the full list of countries and periods available. It also reports summary statistics for the 45 countries in the EDD dataset, using annual averages for the years available from 2006 to 2009. There is significant variation in the number and size of exporters across MENA countries. For example, Yemen has a relatively small number of exporters that are on average small. In contrast, Iran has a relatively large number of exporters that are of a similar size to Yemen's. The same observation holds for the level of diversification at the product and destination level. Exporters in Lebanon are three times more diversified product-wise than their counterparts in Jordan; they also service 60 percent more destinations than exporters in Kuwait. Within countries, we also observe a large difference between the median and the mean values per exporter—the mean values are, on average, 51 times larger than the median values per exporter. This reflects the highly skewed distribution of firms' exports in MENA but around the world more generally.

Table A.1 Exporter-Level Data: Statistics by Country

			Averages computed over 2006–2009				
Region	Country	Period with available data	Number of firms	Average firm size (mn USD)	Share of top 5% firms in annual trade	Average number of products per firm	Average number of destinations per firm
Middle East and North Africa	Egypt, Arab Rep.	2006–2012	8,294	1.8	0.8	4.0	2.6
	Iran, Islamic Rep.	2006–2010	13,171	1.1	0.7	6.1	2.1
	Jordan	2003–2012	1,953	1.9	0.8	2.8	3.1
	Kuwait	2009–2010	3,323	0.9	0.9	4.4	1.9
	Lebanon	2008–2012	5,062	0.7	0.8	7.9	3.1
	Morocco	2002–2012	5,435	2.7	0.7	6.5	2.5
	Yemen, Rep.	2006–2012	512	0.8	0.6	4.7	2.4
Latin America & Caribbean	Brazil	1997–2010	19,107	8.5	0.8		
	Chile	2003–2009	7,248	7.9	0.9	4.6	3.5
	Colombia	2007–2009	9,597	1.9	0.8	4.9	2.8
	Costa Rica	1998–2009	2,899	3.0	0.8	6.0	3.2
	Dominican Rep.	2002–2009	2,784	1.7	0.9	4.8	2.3
	Ecuador	2006–2009	3,195	1.9	0.8	4.3	2.6
	El Salvador	2002–2009	2,558	1.6	0.8	7.0	2.4
	Guatemala	2003–2010	4,454	1.4	0.8	8.2	2.5
	Mexico	2000–2009	33,951	6.5	0.9	7.0	2.2
	Nicaragua	2002–2011	1,247	1.1	0.8	6.2	2.1
	Peru	1997–2009	6,872	3.6	0.9	7.1	2.6

table continues next page

Table A.1 Exporter-Level Data: Statistics by Country *(continued)*

Region	Country	Period with available data	Averages computed over 2006–2009				
			Number of firms	Average firm size (mn USD)	Share of top 5% firms in annual trade	Average number of products per firm	Average number of destinations per firm
Africa	Botswana	2003–2010	1,738	2.4	1.0	6.7	1.4
	Burkina Faso	2005–2010	416	1.3	0.9	3.7	2.3
	Cameroon	1997–2009	1,008	1.8	0.8	4.3	2.7
	Kenya	2006–2009	4,999	0.8	0.8	7.3	2.5
	Malawi	2006–2008	631	1.1	0.9	4.3	1.9
	Mali	2005–2008	306	2.7	0.9	3.8	2.2
	Mauritius	2002–2009	2,232	1.1	0.9	9.1	2.6
	Niger	2008–2010	158	2.3	0.9	4.1	1.5
	Senegal	2000–2010	745	1.3	0.7	6.2	3.3
	South Africa	2001–2009	21,902	2.5	0.9	15.5	3.5
	Tanzania	2003–2009	1,876	1.3	0.9	4.1	2.4
	Uganda	2000–2010	964	1.2	0.8	3.8	2.4
Southeast Europe	Albania	2004–2009	1,944	0.5	0.6	3.2	1.5
	Bulgaria	2001–2006	13,804	0.9	0.8	6.3	2.4
	Macedonia	2001–2010	2,958	0.7	0.8	4.6	2.2
	Turkey	2002–2010	45,133	2.2	0.8	9.8	4.0
Southeast Asia	Cambodia	2000–2009	610	5.0	0.4	7.9	4.8
	Lao PDR	2006–2009	498	1.4	0.9	2.4	1.6
South Asia	Bangladesh	2005–2011	6,552	2.0	0.5	4.3	3.8
	Pakistan	2002–2010	15,181	1.1	0.7	5.4	3.3
Europe	Belgium	1997–2010	22,989	13.1	0.8	9.6	6.9
	Estonia	1997–2009	5,000	1.8	0.7	7.9	2.7
	Norway	1997–2006	18,309	2.1	0.9	5.2	3.4
	New Zealand	1999–2010	13,163	1.8	0.9	7.5	3.1
	Spain	2005–2009	91,233	2.5	0.9	4.7	3.9
	Sweden	1997–2006	30,126	4.3	0.9	6.5	4.3

Exporter Competitiveness Indicators

We exploit the cross-country variation among the 45 countries in the EDD dataset to examine how MENA countries differ from other developing countries in terms of their firms' characteristics, size, diversification patterns, and dynamics. Our analysis makes use of indicators calculated at the country-sector (HS 4-digit)-year obtained from the CYH4.dta file in the EDD. They are defined at the country-(hs4)-year sector level as follows:

1. *Number of exporters$_t$:* Total number of exporting firms in year t.
2. *Average (Median) size of exporter$_t$:* Average (median) export value per exporter in current USD in year t.

3. *Average (standard deviation) number of destinations/products per exporter$_t$:* Average (standard deviation) number of destinations/products served/exported per firm in year t, where products are defined according to the HS Classification at 4 digits and destinations are 246 countries, as described in Cebeci, Fernandes, Freund, and Pierola (2012).

4. *Share of top 5 percent exporters$_t$:* exports of largest 5 percent of exporters$_t$/total exports$_t$. This indicator can be calculated only for countries/sectors with 20 exporters or more.

5. *Entry rate$_t$* = entrants$_t$/number of exporters$_t$, where entrants$_t$ is the number of exporters that are in the sample in year t but not in year t−1.

6. *Exit rate$_t$:* exiters$_t$/number of exporters$_t$, where exiters$_t$ is the number of exporters that are in the sample in year t but not in year t+1.

7. *Share of Entrants$_t$* = total export value of entrants$_t$/total export values of exporters$_t$, where entrants$_t$ are the exporters that are in the sample in year t but not in year t−1.

8. *One-year survival rate$_t$:* stayers$_{t+1}$/entrants$_t$, where stayers$_{t+1}$ is the number of exporters that entered in year t and did not exit therefore they are in the sample in year t+1.

Please note that all indicators have a missing value if the country/sector includes just one exporter.

Data Sources and Access

The firm-level customs data is available to external researchers for several countries including three MENA countries. Table A.2 provides for the MENA countries, more details on the firm-level data, access requirements, and sources.

Table A.2 Firm-Level Data Sources and Access

Economy	Description	Access	Source
Egypt, Arab Rep.	Non-oil export data over the period 2006–2012, by firm product (HS 4-digit) destination country.	Available upon request to the Economic Research Forum Open Access Micro Data Initiative (OAMDI) team	Nonprofit Organization—Economic Research Forum
Iran, Islamic Rep.	Non-oil export data over the period 2006–2010, by firm product (HS 6-digit) destination country.	Restricted	Government—The Islamic Republic of Iran Customs Administration - IRICA
Jordan	Non-oil export data over the period 2003–2012, by firm product (HS 6-digit) destination country.	Available upon request to the World Bank Exporter Dynamics Database team.	Government—Ministry of Planning and International Cooperation and JEDCO
Kuwait	Non-oil export data over the period 2008–2010, by firm product (HS 6-digit) destination country.	Available upon request to the Kuwait customs authority	Government—Kuwait Customs Authority

table continues next page

Table A.2 Firm-Level Data Sources and Access *(continued)*

Economy	Description	Access	Source
Lebanon	Non-oil export data over the period 2008–2010, by firm product (HS 6-digit) destination country.	Available upon request to the Lebanon customs authority	Government—Lebanese Customs Administration
Morocco	Non-oil export data over the period 2002–2012, by firm product (HS 6-digit) destination country.	Available to researchers upon request to the Morocco customs authority	Government—Administration des Douanes et Impôts Indirects
Tunisia	Non-oil export data over the period 2000–2010 by firm product (HS6-digit) destination country; merged with firm panel census data over the period 1997-2010, covering all non-agricultural sectors, no firm-size restrictions.	Accessible onsite and upon request to the Institut National de la Statistique in Tunis	Government—Institut National de la Statistique
West Bank	Firm panel census data for years 2004, 2007 and 2012 and stock market data for the period 2004–2012.	—	Palestine Exchange
Yemen, Rep.	Non-oil export data over the period 2006–2012, by firm product (HS 6-digit) destination country.	Available upon request to the World Bank Exporter Dynamics Database team.	Government—Yemen Customs Authority

Note: — = not available. Non-oil exports cover HS Chapters 01 to 97 excluding HS chapter 27.

We also refer the reader to the Exporter Dynamics Database website (http://microdata.worldbank.org/index.php/catalog/1031) and the Economic Research Forum Open Access Micro Data Initiative website (http://www.erf.org.eg/cms.php?id=erfdataportal) for more information on steps to follow to have access to the firm-level data.

Finally, research papers using the underlying data are available on the following website: http://web.worldbank.org/WBSITE/EXTERNAL/COUNTRIES/MENAEXT/0,,contentMDK:23503794~menuPK:9464020~pagePK:146736~piPK:146830~theSitePK:256299,00.html.

Note

1. See Cebeci et al. (2012) for a detailed description of the data and the cleaning process. A "consolidated" product classification that takes into account the transformations made to product codes according to the HS classification throughout the years was employed. In addition, in order to mitigate the risk of including transactions that correspond to the shipping of samples or personal belongings, we dropped the observations corresponding to exporters that, in a given year, had total sales below $1,000. We also dropped all the observations belonging to chapter 27 according to the HS classification—mineral fuels, oils and product of their distillation, and the like.

Reference

Cebeci, T., A. Fernandes, C. Freund, and M. D. Pierola. 2012. "Exporter Dynamics Database." Working Paper Series 6229, World Bank, Washington, DC.

APPENDIX B

Superstars and Revealed Comparative Advantage across Industries

Table B.1 Superstars and Revealed Comparative Advantage across Industries

Countries' industry	Number of countries with CA sector		Share of country-industries loosing CA in absence of top 1% exporters	
	All (1)	MENA (2)	All (3)	MENA (4)
Superstars driving CA				
Chemicals	5	4	0.8	0.75
Miscellaneous goods	3	0	0.67	n.a.
Electrical machinery	2	0	0.5	n.a.
Metals	13	3	0.46	0.33
Paper	10	3	0.4	0.33
Mineral products	20	5	0.3	0.2
Textiles	15	2	0.13	0
Precious metals	13	2	0.08	0
Superstars not driving CA				
Apparel	18	3	0	0
Food and food products	27	6	0	0
Stone, clay, and glass	8	3	0	0
Plastic and rubber	4	2	0	0
Wood	5	0	0	n.a.
Machinery	0	0	n.a.	n.a.
Transport	1	0	1	n.a.
All (1)	144	33	0.19	0.18
Trade weighted share of (1) in total exports			0.3	0.24

Note: CA = comparative advantage.

NTM Regulatory Distance Methodology

Let i index countries, k HS6 products, and j NTM types as defined by the MAST classification (63 different types of measures). Let n_{ilk} be a dummy variable marking the application of NTM type l by country i on product k. We define "regulatory distance" (RD) at the NTM-product level as $RD_{lk} = |n_{ilk} - n_{jlk}|$. If two countries apply the same measure to the same product, the distance is zero; if they don't, it is one. Finally, let

$$D_{ij} = \frac{1}{N} \sum_k \sum_l |n_{ilk} - n_{jlk}| \tag{1}$$

be the overall regulatory distance between countries i and j, N being the total number of observed product-NTM combinations. Plotting a two-dimensional projection of the regulatory distances D_{ij} gives a "regulatory distance map" where countries close to each other apply NTMs in similar ways across products whereas countries at the graph's periphery apply NTMs in idiosyncratic ways.

Environmental Benefits Statement

The World Bank Group is committed to reducing its environmental footprint. In support of this commitment, the Publishing and Knowledge Division leverages electronic publishing options and print-on-demand technology, which is located in regional hubs worldwide. Together, these initiatives enable print runs to be lowered and shipping distances decreased, resulting in reduced paper consumption, chemical use, greenhouse gas emissions, and waste.

The Publishing and Knowledge Division follows the recommended standards for paper use set by the Green Press Initiative. Whenever possible, books are printed on 50 percent to 100 percent postconsumer recycled paper, and at least 50 percent of the fiber in our book paper is either unbleached or bleached using Totally Chlorine Free (TCF), Processed Chlorine Free (PCF), or Enhanced Elemental Chlorine Free (EECF) processes.

More information about the Bank's environmental philosophy can be found at http://crinfo.worldbank.org/wbcrinfo/node/4.

green press
INITIATIVE